# Black Tie
# and
# Boots Optional

## A Culinary Treasure from
## The Colleyville Woman's Club

### Colleyville, Texas

Underwritten by
**The Dallas Morning News**
Haltom's Jewelers

Photogra~
Dave (
Greg Booth and

The Colleyville Woman's Club is a non-profit organization dedicated to the pursuit of education, philanthropic, and social goals in the community. Members build friendship, participate in activities and, through fund raising and volunteer service, contribute to the welfare of the community. Proceeds from Black Tie and Boots Optional will support many worthwhile philanthropic endeavors in our community.

Printed in the USA by

**WIMMER**

The Wimmer Companies

Memphis

1-800-548-2537

# Committee

| | |
|---|---|
| Chair | Judith Eulberg |
| Co-Chair | Debra Schneider |
| Co-Chair | Lynda Sanders |
| Editor | Jean Neisius |
| Marketing Coordinator | Mary McClain |
| Recipe Coordinators | Cathy Gordon |
| | Jane Nelson |
| Menu Coordinator | Sandie Fouke |
| Food Stylists | Lynda Sanders |
| | Mary MacDowell |
| | Sandie Fouke |
| Artists | Debbie Smith |
| | Lonna Souther |
| | Christine Pasienski |
| Secretary | Janet Smith |
| Treasurer | Patti Irwin |
| Typing Coordinator | Billie Jo Runyon |

## Committee Members

| | |
|---|---|
| Mary Andrews | Janice Kane |
| Barbara Antczak | Judy Lemke |
| Carole Battist | Susan Loftis |
| Mary Beadles | Carol Logan |
| Janet Cady | Yvonne Mason |
| Karen Cantrell | Jane McKain |
| Sheila Carter | Susan Miller |
| Kay Craft | Bonnie Pasienski |
| Terry Cosmano | Carol Provost |
| Nancy Dennis | Vivian Quatro |
| Joyce DeSarno | Shirley Schollmeyer |
| Judy Duncan | Cristal Smith |
| Rachel Eulberg (mascot) | Judith Wills |
| Gloria Flores | Cindy Woelke |
| Diane Foia | Carol Wollin |
| Suzanne Harrington | Maurine Wood |
| Sue Howery | |

# Introduction

The Colleyville Woman's Club, an organization of about 300 members, serves primarily charitable and educational functions. Originally founded in 1978 as the Colleyville Newcomer's Club, the group has evolved from a small group of new residents into an organization dedicated to community service. Through its fund raisers, it supports such causes as the Women's Haven of Tarrant County, Women's Shelter of Arlington, GRACE (a community short-term and emergency relief association), Meals on Wheels, and numerous other charities. For many years, it has encouraged volunteerism in the area's young people by sponsoring a Youth Recognition Awards Ceremony. The club's theme, Circle of Hope, reflects its commitment to a broad range of philanthropic and community events.

The Colleyville Woman's Club holds several fund raisers a year for the exclusive purpose of supporting charitable causes. While the club raises funds through several means, its most visible events are the Holiday Home Tour, the Annual Spring Fashion Show, and the cookbook. *Black Tie and Boots Optional* is actually CWC's second cookbook, *A Taste of Tradition* having preceded it in 1985.

Why black tie and boots optional and what does it have to do with a suburban Texas women's club? Colleyville, located midway between Dallas and Fort Worth, serves the metropolitan area as a "bedroom community," and in turn is served by both cities. While some of us are native Texans and are deeply rooted in Texas soil, more often we have been transplanted from many different areas of the world. Along with diverse customs and dialects, we have brought with us a considerable variety of foods. When we gather for a social event, our tables reflect the diversity of our backgrounds. We have grown to love our adopted area and have incorporated Texas and its culinary customs into our lives. We have learned to cook with cilantro and even to appreciate jalapeño chilies (some of us have learned the hard way to wear gloves when we work with these hot foods). We know that corn meal comes in blue in addition to the better known yellow and white, and we appreciate margaritas on a hot summer evening.

Again, why black tie and boots? Texas is indeed a world of its own (incidentally, the only state in the union to have ever been a republic of its own). Our world is big, casual, glitzy, sophisticated, down-home, and proud, but above all it is generous and big-hearted. When a Texan goes "black tie," he is as likely to wear his boots with his tuxedo and diamond studs as he is to wear patent leather pumps. His bejeweled "lady," on the other hand, will be decked out in her best sequined long gown, possibly purchased at that legendary department store so closely associated with Dallas. Life in our part of the world includes everything from a casual day at an armadillo hunt or a child's soccer game to a black tie reception at the symphony or at one of our marvelous museums. We work hard and play hard, caring deeply for our children, our homes, and our community. We play golf, fight fire ants, garden, support youth activities, and care for those who are less fortunate than we might be. Whether we are native grown or transplants, we are proud to be Texans and proud to offer you our best culinary efforts.

# Table of Contents

Menus:

From Boots
to
Black Tie

# Our Menus

No one will dispute that life in the late twentieth century is busy. We hold jobs, rear children, participate in community activities, and maintain a social life—an incredible balancing act for most of us. However, we still enjoy getting together with friends and entertaining family and acquaintances, and invariably on these social occasions, we like the community activity of sharing a meal.

While we all tend to entertain during the traditional holiday seasons, in Black Tie and Boots Optional we have chosen instead to base our menus on the events of our lives that call for food in addition to Christmas and Thanksgiving.

One of the best features of our community is the atmosphere it provides for our children. Whether we are coaching their soccer games, cheering at the traditional Friday night high school football game from packed stands, or recognizing our young volunteers at CWC's annual Youth Recognition Awards Ceremony, we seem to include food.

As part of the metropolitan "mid-cities," Colleyville is bordered by several towns, two of which celebrate unique festivals of their own. Euless's Arbor Daze celebration has become a spring weekend fair that appeals to the whole family. Neighboring Grapevine has become well known for its young wine industry, celebrated with Grapefest in the fall (our Harvest of the Vines).

Because we do not live near the seashore and it gets rather warm in Texas in the summer, many of us have swimming pools, hence the "cement pond" as a scene of many of our warm weather social events. And as any resident of our area knows, we watch out for our fierce fire ants before we spread a blanket for a picnic in the summer (isn't everything bigger in Texas).

Some may call it "road kill," but the armadillo is one symbol of the indomitable Texas spirit.

And yes, seasons do change, often from day to day, and it does get cold in Texas (just watch a Texan try to drive on ice when we get our annual ice storm), so a romantic dinner for two in front of a roaring fire, even if it does emanate from gas logs, might be another part of our lives.

Like people everywhere, we give wedding and baby showers, have Super Bowl parties, and entertain new neighbors. We give cocktail parties and have dessert parties after an evening event.

And like people the world over, we like to share the events of our lives with the communion of good food. With great pleasure, therefore, we share with you some of the menus we enjoy as part of our lives in our own "big little" part of the world.

## Soccer Mom Scores

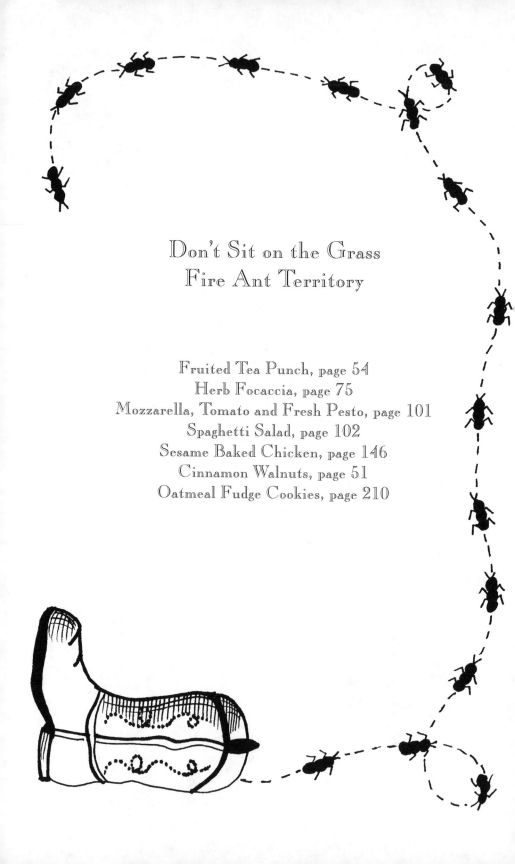

Don't Sit on the Grass
Fire Ant Territory

# Armadillo Hunt Brunch

Tampico Fizz, page 53
Prosciutto-Wrapped Asparagus, page 32
Tortilla Egg Scramble, page 62
or
Eggs Portugal, page 68
Cherry Tomato Appetizers, page 28
Garlic Cheese Grits, page 60
Apple Cinnamon French Toast, page 66
Angel Biscuits, page 81
Lemon Chess Pie, page 241
Peach Raspberry Batter Cake, page 232
or
Bourbon Pecan Pound Cake, page 237

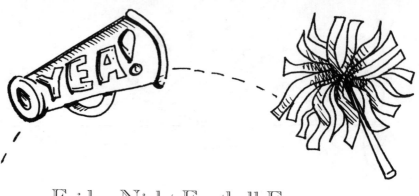

# Friday Night Football Frenzy

Party Fruit Punch, page 52
Chili Popcorn, page 52
Conqueso Dip and Chips
Southwestern Grilled Chicken Salad, page 110
Pretzel Jello, page 103
Hot Ham Happy Sandwiches, page 68
or
Calzones (Quick and Easy), page 122
or
Italian Beef on Hoagies, page 123
Caramel Bananas, page 217
Treasure Chest Bars, page 210
Meringue Cookies, page 212

# Souper Sunday

Black Bean and Rice, St. Louis Style, page 178
Chicken-White Bean Soup, page 91
Cornbread
or
One Minute Bread, page 82
Tossed Green Salad
Hummingbird Cake
with Cream Cheese Frosting, page 235
Crisp Red Apples

# Bloom Where You're Planted
## (New Neighbor Brunch)

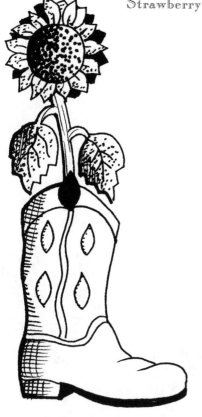

# A Leafy Sensation
## (Arbor Day)

Fruited Tea Punch, page 54
Oriental Chicken Salad, page 113
Perfecto Pasta Salad, page 117
Spinach Salad with
Creamy Mustard Dressing, page 106
Rich Refrigerator Rolls, page 78
Sesame Butter, page 119
Fruit Curd Tartlets, page 221
Quick, Easy and Sinfully
Rich Chocolate Cake, page 240

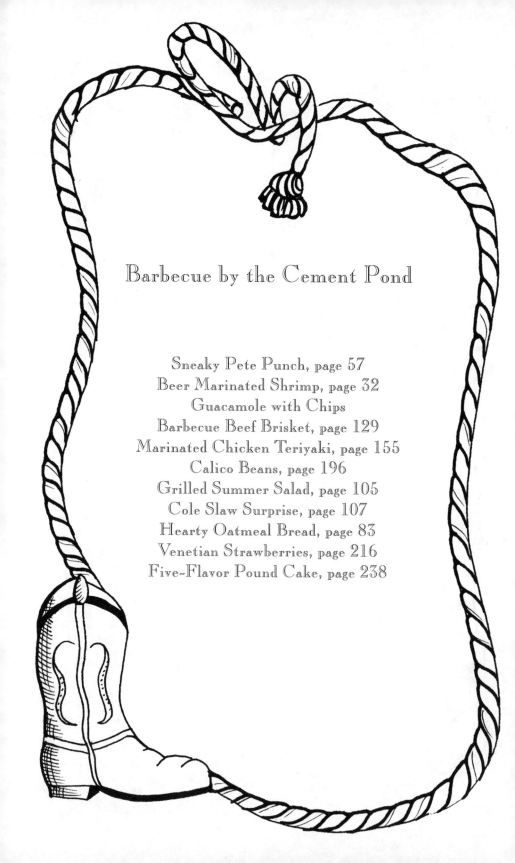

# Barbecue by the Cement Pond

Too Hot to Handle
(Texas Independence Day)

Sausage Cheese Balls, page 47
Crabmeat Cheesecake, page 35
Tortilla Soup, page 90
Chicken Chili Lime Soup, page 97
First Prize Caesar Salad, page 104
or
Black Bean and Corn Salad
served in Tomato Cups, page 108
Marinated Pork Tenderloin
with Jicama Salsa, page 138
Blue Corn Muffins, page 74
Flan, page 222
Margarita Pie, page 242

# Icebound by the Gas Logs
## (Winter Candlelight Dinner for Two)

Mushroom Pâté, page 44
Cornish Hens with Fruit Stuffing, page 147
Asparagus Parmigiano, page 203
Praline Sweet Potato Casserole, page 197
Kiss Me Rolls, page 77

or

Herbed Bubble Bread, page 77
Pavlova, page 214

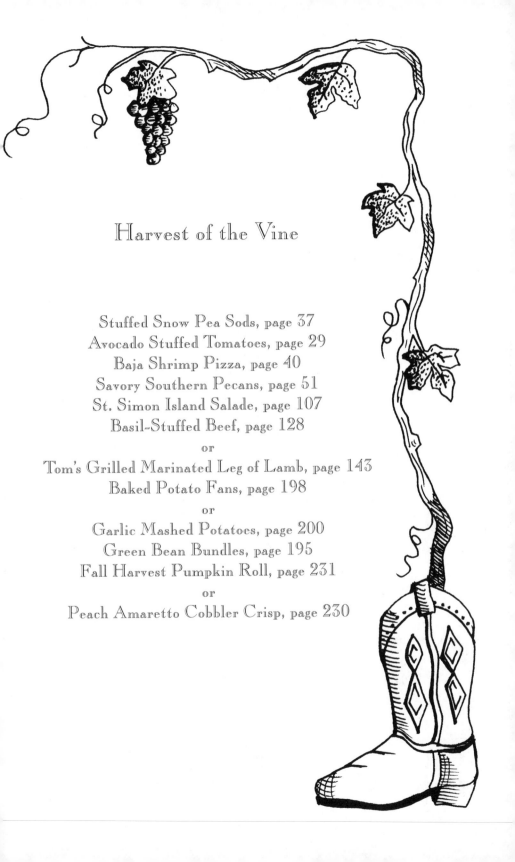

# Harvest of the Vine

Stuffed Snow Pea Sods, page 37
Avocado Stuffed Tomatoes, page 29
Baja Shrimp Pizza, page 40
Savory Southern Pecans, page 51
St. Simon Island Salade, page 107
Basil-Stuffed Beef, page 128

or

Tom's Grilled Marinated Leg of Lamb, page 143
Baked Potato Fans, page 198

or

Garlic Mashed Potatoes, page 200
Green Bean Bundles, page 195
Fall Harvest Pumpkin Roll, page 231

or

Peach Amaretto Cobbler Crisp, page 230

## Linens, Ribbons and Lingerie

# The Boss Is Coming to Dinner

Artichoke with Seafood and Jack Cheese, page 27
Gazpacho Blanco, page 97
Pear Walnut Salad, page 108
Crusted Salmon with Herbed Mayonnaise, page 160
Spinach Feta Casserole, page 192
Wild Rice with
Mushrooms and Almonds, page 176
French Bread, page 86
Mocha-Orange Cheesecake Royale, page 226
Assorted Cheeses

# Black Tie and Boots Optional

Cucumber Rounds
with Smoked Salmon Mousse, page 27
Basil Sun-Dried Tomato Spread, page 44
Coconut-Beer Shrimp, page 33
Sherry Baked Brie, page 46
Filet with Snow Peas
and Mustard Caper Sauce, page 36
Chicken Liver Paté
with Port Wine Aspic, page 48
Spinach Bacon Spread, page 26
Crabmeat Cheese Mounds, page 26
Olive-Cheese Puffs, page 37
Spinach Phyllo Triangles, page 38
Chinese Barbecue Pork, page 136
Cream Puffs, page 218
White Chocolate Tamales, page 231
Kahlúa and Praline Brownies, page 244
Ebony and Ivory
Chocolate Truffles, page 233
Swedish Nut Balls, page 211

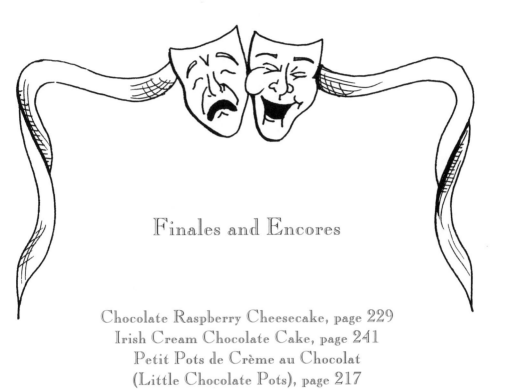

# Finales and Encores

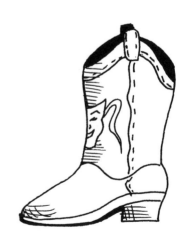

Appetizers
and
Beverages

# Crabmeat Cheese Mounds

1    loaf of French bread, sliced into ¼-inch slices
1    stick butter or margarine
1    (4 ounce) can green chilies, chopped and drained
     garlic salt to taste
1    (6 ounce) can crabmeat
1    cup mayonnaise
8    ounces shredded cheddar cheese

Place French bread slices on cookie sheet and toast until golden brown.

Mix together the butter, green chilies and garlic salt. Spread on toasted slices.

Mix together crabmeat, mayonnaise and cheddar cheese. Mound on toast slices on top of butter mixture (can be frozen at this point). When ready to serve, place under broiler until bubbly.

# Spinach Bacon Spread

8    slices bacon, cooked and crumbled
2    (10 ounce) packages frozen chopped spinach, thawed and drained
4    (8 ounce) packages Monterey Jack cheese with jalapeño peppers, shredded
1    (11 ounce) can condensed cheddar cheese soup, undiluted
1    (8 ounce) package cream cheese, softened
1    teaspoon Greek seasoning
½    teaspoon onion powder
1    teaspoon hot sauce
1    (2 ounce) jar diced pimiento, drained
     paprika (optional)

Combine first eight ingredients in lightly greased 11x7x1½-inch baking dish; microwave on high 3 minutes, and then at 50% power for 7-9 minutes, stirring every 1½ minutes. Sprinkle mixture with pimiento and paprika. Serve with crackers or bagel chips.

# Artichoke with Seafood and Jack Cheese

| | |
|---|---|
| 2 | fresh artichokes |
| ½ | cup peeled and deveined shrimp |
| ½ | cup bay scallops |
| ¼ | cup crabmeat |
| 1 | cup champagne |
| 3 | tablespoons melted butter |
| 1 | tablespoon fresh chopped garlic |
| ½ | diced onion |
| 1 | teaspoon dried basil |
| 1 | teaspoon dried oregano |
| ½ | teaspoon marjoram |
| 2 | cups shredded Monterey Jack cheese |
| | salt and pepper to taste |

Boil two fresh artichokes about 15 minutes. Cool. Slice in half and remove purple center area. Set aside. In a two quart saucepan heat butter, garlic, onion until garlic starts to brown. Add shrimp, scallops and crabmeat. Cook on high heat for five minutes. Pour in champagne and add one cup of Monterey Jack cheese. Reduce to medium heat until mixture thickens. Remove from heat and stir in basil, oregano and marjoram. Place artichokes in a baking dish and pour mixture over artichokes. Top with remaining Jack cheese and place in oven at 350 degrees until cheese starts to brown. Serves 4

# Cucumber Rounds with Smoked Salmon Mousse

| | |
|---|---|
| 1 | (8 ounce) package cream cheese at room temperature |
| 2 | ounces smoked salmon |
| 3 | tablespoons heavy cream |
| ¼ | teaspoon lemon juice |
| 2 | seedless English cucumbers |

Combine cream cheese, salmon, cream and lemon juice in the bowl of food processor and blend until smooth. Chill 30 minutes. Slice cucumbers crosswise into twenty slices. Make a small hollow for the filling in the center and use a piping bag filled with cream cheese mixture and pipe each cucumber center. May be made up to an hour before serving. Makes 1¼ cups or approximately 40 hors d'oeuvres

# Shrimp Balls with Cocktail Sauce

| | |
|---|---|
| 1 | pound shrimp, peeled, deveined and minced |
| ½ | cup chopped water chestnuts |
| 1 | egg white |
| ½ | teaspoon salt |
| 1 | teaspoon cornstarch |
| 1 | teaspoon sherry |
| ½ | teaspoon fresh minced ginger root |
| ¼ | teaspoon sugar |
| | dash freshly ground pepper |
| | vegetable oil |

Combine all ingredients except oil. Chill one hour or more. Shape mixture into balls with a teaspoon. To deep fry, heat oil to 375 degrees and fry until golden. To pan fry, sauté balls in oil until golden. Drain on paper toweling. Serve shrimp balls warm with hot mustard, plum sauce or cocktail sauce. Makes 24 appetizers

# Cocktail Sauce

| | |
|---|---|
| 1 | cup catsup |
| 1½ | tablespoons Old Bay seasoning |
| ½ | teaspoon brown sugar |
| ½ | teaspoon horseradish |

Combine all ingredients and chill. Serve with shrimp balls.

# Cherry Tomato Appetizers

| | |
|---|---|
| 1 | pint cherry tomatoes |
| ⅓ | pound cream cheese |
| ⅓ | cup sour cream |
| 1 | teaspoon lemon juice |
| | pinch salt |
| | dash hot pepper sauce |
| | paprika, for garnish |
| | parsley, for garnish |

Wash tomatoes, cut off tomato tops, and scoop out pulp. Drain well.

Mix remaining ingredients. Stuff tomatoes with mixture. Garnish with paprika and parsley. Serve chilled. Makes 24 appetizers

*May add crabmeat or shrimp.*

*Photo on right ~*
Baja Shrimp Pizza, page 40

# Della Robbia Wreath

2 Red Delicious apples
2 Granny Smith apples
2 Golden Delicious apples
2 (8 ounce) packages cream cheese, softened
4 tablespoons powdered sugar
1 teaspoon curry powder
⅔ cup flaked sweetened coconut
⅔ cup finely chopped pecans
6 maraschino cherry halves
12 pecan halves
lemon juice

Combine cream cheese, sugar, curry, coconut and half of the pecans.

Line a three-cup ring mold with plastic wrap and pack cheese mixture in and chill thoroughly, at least four hours or overnight.

When ready to serve, remove ring from mold and remove plastic wrap. Press remaining ⅓ cup pecans into cheese ring.

Cut apples in wedges, leaving skins on. Dip in lemon juice to prevent discoloring and place apple wedges around edge of mold, skin side up, in alternating colors and sticking point of apple into mold. Garnish ring with maraschino cherry halves and pecans. Serves 12

# Avocado Stuffed Tomatoes

1 pint red or yellow cherry tomatoes
1 large ripe avocado
2 scallions, minced, including green tops
1 tablespoon lemon juice
½ teaspoon cumin
dash hot pepper sauce
4 slices crisp cooked bacon, crumbled

Remove a thin slice from top of each tomato. Scoop out pulp. Drain upside down on paper toweling 30 minutes. Mash avocado coarsely with fork. Stir in scallions, lemon juice, cumin, and hot pepper sauce. May add more lemon, cumin, and hot pepper sauce to taste. Fill tomato with avocado mixture. Top with bacon pieces. Makes 24 appetizers

*Photo on left ~*
Friday Night Football
Frenzy, page 12

# Goat Cheese Tart

2 medium-size red onions, unpeeled, each cut into 12 wedges
3 tablespoons olive oil
1 sheet frozen puff pastry (half of 17¼ ounce package), thawed
1 large egg, beaten to blend
8 ounces soft fresh goat cheese (such as Montrachet)
¼ cup purchased pesto
¼ cup whipping cream
3 tablespoons chopped fresh basil

Preheat oven to 400 degrees. Oil heavy large baking sheet. Toss onion wedges with oil in medium bowl. Season with salt and pepper. Arrange onions in single layer on baking sheet and bake until very tender with golden bottoms, about 25 minutes. Transfer sheet to rack; cool. Cover and let stand at room temperature. (Can be made 1 day ahead.)

Preheat oven to 400 degrees. Roll out pastry on lightly floured surface to 14x11-inch rectangle. Trim edges to even. Cut ½ inch strip from each side of pastry, forming 13x10-inch rectangle; reserve strips.

Transfer pastry rectangle to another heavy large baking sheet. Brush edges with some of beaten egg; reserve remaining egg. Place strips on edges of tart, creating border. Trim strips; press gently to adhere. Pierce bottom of pastry several times with fork. Bake until edges puff and pastry is golden brown, about 15 minutes. Transfer baking sheet to rack.

Using metal spatula, loosen pastry from baking sheet. Cool completely on sheet. Reduce oven temperature to 350 degrees.

Stir cheese, pesto, cream and 2 tablespoons basil in medium bowl until smooth. Season with salt and pepper. Mix in remaining beaten egg. Spread cheese mixture evenly over bottom of crust.

*(continued on next page)*

*(Goat Cheese Tart continued)*

Remove peel and stem end from roasted onions. Fan wedges, golden brown side up, over cheese mixture.

Bake tart until crust is brown and cheese appears set, about 20 minutes. Transfer baking sheet to rack and cool tart to room temperature. Sprinkle tart with remaining 1 tablespoon basil. Cut into squares. Serves 10

# Herbed Seafood Bruschetta

3    tablespoons olive oil, divided
1    tablespoon lemon juice
1    tablespoon snipped chives
1    tablespoon snipped fresh basil
1    tablespoon snipped fresh mint
1    teaspoon bottled minced garlic
1    (6 ounce) package frozen crabmeat, thawed and drained, or one (6.5 ounce) can crabmeat, drained, flaked and cartilage removed
8    ounces peeled, deveined, and cooked shrimp, coarsely chopped
1    cup chopped plum tomatoes
½    cup finely chopped onion
1    (8 ounce) loaf French bread (baguette)
     freshly ground pepper
     fresh chives (optional)

In a mixing bowl stir together 1 tablespoon olive oil, lemon juice, chives, basil, mint, and garlic. Add crabmeat, shrimp, plum tomatoes, and onion; toss to coat. Cut the baguette into 48 thin slices; brush one side of each slice with remaining olive oil; sprinkle lightly with pepper.

Arrange bread, brushed side up, on baking sheet. Broil 3 to 4 inches from heat for 1 to 2 minutes or until lightly toasted. Arrange, oiled side up. On a serving platter; spoon seafood mixture on toast rounds.

If desired, garnish with fresh chives. Serve at once. Makes 48 appetizers

# Prosciutto-Wrapped Asparagus

| | |
|---|---|
| 12 | stalks of asparagus |
| 4 | thin slices of prosciutto |
| 4 | pats unsalted butter |
| | freshly ground pepper |
| ½ | cup freshly grated Italian Parmesan cheese |
| 1 | lemon, quartered |

Cut off tough ends of asparagus; cover asparagus with water in a skillet; bring to a boil and cook until tender, but still firm (3-4 minutes). Drain well. Divide asparagus into four bundles of three stalks each; wrap prosciutto slice around center of bundle. Place the four bundles into an oven proof dish; dot with butter; season with pepper and sprinkle with Parmesan cheese.

Bake at 350 degrees for 4-5 minutes to brown the cheese. Serve with lemon wedges. Makes 4 appetizers

# Beer Marinated Shrimp

| | |
|---|---|
| 2 | pounds shrimp |
| 3 | cups beer |
| 1 | cup water |
| 2½ | teaspoons salt, divided |
| ⅔ | cup oil |
| ½ | cup white tarragon vinegar |
| ¼ | cup fresh chopped parsley |
| ½ | teaspoon hot pepper sauce |
| | dash ground black pepper |
| 1 | onion, sliced very thin |
| 2 | lemons, sliced very thin |
| 2 | tablespoons capers with liquid |

Boil shrimp in beer, water and 1 teaspoon salt until shrimp is pink. Drain shrimp and peel. In a small jar with lid, combine oil, vinegar, parsley, 1½ teaspoons salt, pepper and hot pepper sauce. Cover and shake well. In a large glass bowl, alternate layers of shrimp, onion slices, and lemon slices. Pour oil and vinegar mixture over all. Marinate in refrigerator for at least eight hours. Serve with toothpicks. Makes 12 appetizers

# Coconut-Beer Shrimp

| | |
|---|---|
| 1 | pound medium fresh shrimp |
| 2¼ | teaspoons red pepper |
| 1⅛ | teaspoons salt |
| 1 | teaspoon pepper |
| ¾ | teaspoon paprika |
| ½ | teaspoon garlic powder |
| ½ | teaspoon onion powder |
| ½ | teaspoon thyme |
| ½ | teaspoon oregano |
| ¾ | cup, plus 2 tablespoons, all-purpose flour |
| ¼ | cup, plus 2 tablespoons, beer |
| 1 | egg, beaten |
| ½ | teaspoon baking powder |
| 1 | (7 ounce) package flaked coconut |
| | vegetable oil |

Peel and devein shrimp, leaving tails on; rinse well, and set aside.

Combine seasonings in a small bowl, mixing well; set aside. Combine flour, beer, egg, and baking powder in a medium bowl; mix well.

Dip shrimp into seasoning mixture, shake off excess mixture. Dip seasoned shrimp into beer batter. Dredge batter-coated shrimp in coconut.

Fry shrimp, 5-6 at a time, in deep, hot oil (350 degrees) about 45 seconds on each side or until golden brown. Drain on paper towels, and serve with Spicy Orange Dip.

## Spicy Orange Dip

| | |
|---|---|
| 1 | (10 ounce) jar orange marmalade |
| 3 | tablespoons prepared horseradish |
| 3 | tablespoons spicy brown mustard |
| ½ | teaspoon grated lemon rind |

Combine all ingredients and mix well. Chill.

# Crabmeat "Pizza"

2 (8 ounce) packages cream cheese
2 tablespoons Worcestershire sauce
1 tablespoon fresh lemon juice
2 tablespoons mayonnaise
1 small onion, grated extra fine
2 shakes garlic salt
1 bottle chili sauce
1 (6½ ounce) can minced crabmeat
dried parsley
horseradish to taste

Drain crabmeat; pick through to remove any small bits of shell. Rinse with cold water and drain very well. Fluff well with fork. Set aside.

Mix cream cheese, Worcestershire sauce, lemon juice, mayonnaise, onion and garlic salt until well blended. Spread on round 12 inch platter, about ½ inch thick.

Combine chili sauce and horseradish to taste. Spread ¾ of the mixture over the cream cheese, to within an inch of the rim, resembling a pizza. Sprinkle crabmeat over the chili layer, taking care to stay within the border. Cover platter to the edge with a generous, heavy layer of dried parsley. The dried parsley will absorb any excess moisture from crabmeat.

Cover with plastic wrap; refrigerate overnight.

To serve, remove the plastic and use a paper towel to carefully blot any excess moisture not absorbed by the parsley. Serve with crackers and a knife for spreading. Serves 12

*This must be prepared ahead of time; does not freeze well.*

# Beef Rolls

1   (6 ounce) package cream cheese, softened
3   teaspoons grated onions
2   teaspoons horseradish
4   ounces sliced beef
    dash Worcestershire sauce

Combine cream cheese, onion, horseradish and Worcestershire. Mix well.

Spread mixture on one slice of beef at a time. Roll beef up and refrigerate.

When thoroughly chilled, cut the beef rolls into bite size pieces.

# Crabmeat Cheesecake

1   cup buttery cracker crumbs (25-30 crackers)
3   tablespoons butter, melted
2   (8 ounce) packages cream cheese, softened
3   large eggs
¾   cup sour cream, divided
2   teaspoons onion, grated
1   teaspoon lemon juice
½   teaspoon hot sauce
¼   teaspoon freshly ground pepper
⅛   teaspoon cayenne pepper
⅛   teaspoon red pepper flakes
1   cup fresh crabmeat, drained and flaked (canned may be used, if necessary)
1   tablespoon chopped chives or green onion

Combine cracker crumbs and butter. Firmly press crumb mixture on bottom of an ungreased 9-inch springform pan. Bake at 350 degrees for ten minutes; let cool on a wire rack.

Beat cream cheese, eggs, and ¼ cup sour cream at medium speed of an electric mixer until creamy. Add onion, lemon juice, hot sauce, and spices; beat well. Stir in crabmeat. Pour into prepared pan.

Bake, uncovered, at 325 degrees for 50 minutes or until center is almost set.

Gently run a knife around edge of pan to release sides. Let cool in pan on wire rack. Carefully remove sides of springform pan.

Spread remaining ½ cup sour cream over top. Sprinkle top with chives or green onions.

*May be used as an entrée.*

# Filet and Snow Peas with Mustard Caper Sauce

1   (2½ pound) beef tender-
    loin
1   tablespoon cracked black
    pepper
1   tablespoon walnut oil
2   tablespoons good bourbon
¼   pound snow pea pods
    Mustard-Caper Sauce

Preheat oven to 425 degrees. Trim the filet of any fat and tie it closed with cotton string. Roll the meat in the cracked pepper. Heat the oil in a heavy sauté pan or skillet. Add the filet and brown on all sides. Pour the bourbon into the pan and light with a match. After the alcohol burns off, remove the filet to a roasting pan and roast until medium rare, approximately 20 minutes. Let cool and slice as thinly as possible.

Cook the snow peas in a large amount of boiling salted water for one minute, then drain and plunge into cold water. Drain the peas again, remove the strings and ends, and split the peas in half.

Wrap a bite-sized piece of filet in half a snow pea and close with a toothpick. Serve with Mustard Caper Sauce. Makes 50 appetizers

## Mustard-Caper Sauce

4   egg yolks
3   tablespoons Dijon mus-
    tard
2   teaspoons fresh lemon
    juice
⅓   bunch fresh chives,
    snipped
½   cup olive oil
½   cup heavy cream
2   tablespoons capers,
    drained
    salt and pepper to taste

Put the yolks in a blender or food processor with the mustard, lemon juice and chives, and blend. Add the oil in a thin steady stream with the machine running. Stop and scrape down the sides. Add the cream the same way. Add the capers and blend slightly. Season to taste.

36

# Stuffed Snow Pea Pods

| | |
|---|---|
| 50 | whole snow pea pods |
| 1 | (8 ounce) package cream cheese, softened |
| 6 | tablespoons tomato puree |
| 6 | teaspoons mayonnaise |
| ½ | teaspoon dry mustard |
| ¼ | teaspoon powdered coriander |
| | salt |
| | white pepper |

Pour boiling salted water over snow pea pods and let soak for one minute. Drain and dry the pods. While still warm, make an incision ¼-inch long across the width in the flat side of each pod. Using a sharp pointed knife, cut through just to the inside of the pod. The opposite side must not be cut. Cool the pods.

Blend cream cheese with tomato puree, mayonnaise, dry mustard, coriander, salt and pepper. Using a metal cake decorator fitted with a small plain tube, pipe the mixture into the pea pods through the incision.

Chill the pods for at least an hour before serving. Makes 50 appetizers

# Olive-Cheese Puffs

| | |
|---|---|
| 2 | cups grated sharp cheese |
| ½ | cup butter, softened |
| ½ | teaspoon salt |
| 1 | cup flour |
| 1 | teaspoon paprika |
| | dash cayenne pepper |
| 50 | small stuffed green olives |

Blend cheese with salt and butter; stir in flour and seasonings (which have been sifted). Wrap one teaspoon of mixture around each olive.

Chill until firm or freeze.

Bake on baking sheet at 400 degrees for 15 minutes. Makes 50 appetizers

37

# Spinach Phyllo Triangles

1 (10 ounce) package frozen chopped spinach, thawed
½ cup onion, chopped
1 clove garlic, minced
6 ounces feta cheese, finely crumbled
½ teaspoon dried oregano, crushed
12 sheets phyllo dough (8 to 10 ounces)
½ cup margarine or butter, melted

Preheat oven to 375 degrees.

For filling, cook spinach according to spinach package directions. Drain well in colander. Press the back of a spoon against mixture to force out excess moisture. Add onion and garlic.

Combine spinach mixture, feta cheese, and oregano. Lightly brush one sheet of phyllo with some of the melted margarine or butter. Place another phyllo sheet on top; brush with some margarine. Repeat with a third sheet of phyllo and margarine. Cover remaining phyllo with a damp cloth to prevent drying.

Cut the stack of phyllo lengthwise into six strips. For each triangle, spoon about 1 tablespoon of the filling about one inch from one end of each strip. Fold the end over the filling at a 45-degree angle. Continue folding to form a triangle that encloses the filling. Repeat with remaining phyllo, margarine or butter, and filling.

Place triangles on a baking sheet. Brush with margarine.

Bake at 375 degrees for 18-20 minutes or until golden brown. Makes 24 appetizers

# Eggroll Shanghai

1 pound ground pork
1 pound ground beef
1 pound cooked shrimp
   (optional)
2 medium carrots, finely
   shredded
1 medium onion, finely
   chopped
   garlic salt and pepper to
   taste
1 egg, unbeaten
1 tablespoon soy sauce
1 package thin eggroll
   wrapper
   vegetable oil

Mix first five ingredients well. Season with salt and pepper.

Add whole unbeaten egg and soy sauce. Spread 1 tablespoon of mixture all over the eggroll wrapper and wrap to a cigar-size diameter. Cut in half. Deep fry in hot oil.

Serve with hot and spicy sweet and sour sauce.

# Josephinas

4 ounces diced mild green
   chiles
1 stick butter, softened to
   room temperature
1 cup mayonnaise
2 cups grated Monterey
   Jack cheese
2 loaves small diameter
   French bread
   parsley sprigs

In a medium-sized bowl, mix chiles with butter, mayonnaise and cheese until well blended.

Slice bread into thin slices and spread amply with the mixture, making sure to completely cover the bread. Place slices on an ungreased cookie sheet in a preheated broiler and broil for 5 to 10 minutes until spread is bubbly. Serve on a large platter garnished with parsley sprigs. Serves 10-12

*May be kept covered in refrigerator for up to one week.*
*May use low fat or non-fat mayonnaise and any low fat cheese; pimientos instead of chilies. May add chopped green or black olives, and chopped onions.*

# Baja Shrimp Pizza

8  ounces Monterey Jack
   cheese, grated
1  pizza crust (recipe follows) or (16 ounce)
   purchased pizza crust
1  large red onion, peeled,
   thinly sliced, and
   caramelized or ½ cup
   thinly sliced red onion
1  small jalapeño pepper,
   cored, seeded, and
   finely chopped
¾  pound shrimp, cooked,
   peeled, and deveined
½  pound fresh mushrooms,
   sliced
3  Italian plum tomatoes,
   quartered
¼  cup chopped fresh cilantro
2  tablespoons Italian salad
   dressing, homemade or
   purchased

Preheat oven to 425 degrees.
Sprinkle cheese over pizza crust and
top with red onion and jalapeño.
Arrange shrimp in a spiral design on
top and sprinkle with mushrooms.
Arrange tomatoes on top and
sprinkle with cilantro and Italian
dressing. Bake for 10-15 minutes.
Serves 4 as main dish or 8 appetizers

Pizza Crust

1  (¼ ounce) package dry
   yeast
¼  cup warm (105-115
   degrees) water
3  cups flour
1  teaspoon salt
2  tablespoons olive oil
1  tablespoon honey
¾  cup cold water

In small glass bowl, dissolve yeast in
warm water and let stand 10 minutes,
until slightly bubbly.

In large bowl, combine flour, salt,
olive oil, honey, and cold water. Add
yeast mixture and stir to blend.
Knead by hand until smooth and
glossy, about 10 minutes. Form into
ball and place dough in oiled bowl,
turning to coat entire surface.

Cover with plastic wrap and towel
and let rise until doubled in bulk,
about 1 hour.

*(continued on next page)*

Preheat oven to 450 degrees. Divide in half and shape each piece into a 12-inch round. (May be prepared to this point up to 2 months in advance. Place dough in freezer-safe plastic bag and freeze. Thaw, at room temperature, 30 minutes before proceeding.)

Crust may be prebaked 10 minutes before adding toppings, or top uncooked crust with desired toppings and bake 10-15 minutes, or until crust is golden brown.

# Crawfish Pie

| | |
|---|---|
| 1 | tablespoon lemon juice |
| 1 | pound crawfish tails |
| ½ | cup chopped green onions |
| ½ | cup fresh parsley, chopped |
| 2 | tablespoons butter, melted |
| 2 | cloves garlic, chopped |
| 1 | tablespoon seafood seasoning |
| ⅓ | cup heavy cream |
| 3 | tablespoons Parmesan cheese |
| ¼ | cup dry vermouth |
| 1 | sheet frozen puffed pastry, thawed |
| ½ | pound Gouda cheese, sliced thin |

Cover pastry sheet with a cloth or plastic wrap and let thaw.

Simmer lemon juice, crawfish, onions, parsley, butter, garlic, and seasoning until heated through.

Add cream, Parmesan cheese, and vermouth. Simmer until liquid is consumed into other ingredients and reduced. Cool.

Roll out pastry sheet and place in pie pan with 4-5 inches hanging over the edge. Layer Gouda cheese and crawfish mixture in shell. Fold edges into the center, pinching any openings together. Gather center of dough into a knot.

Bake at 350 degrees for 30 minutes. Serves 8-10

*Can be used as a main dish or as an appetizer. This is an old Louisiana favorite.*

# Layered Mexican Dip (Low Fat)

2   (1 pound) cans fat free refried beans
½   pound ground turkey, cooked and drained
3   cups nonfat mozzarella cheese
1   cup low fat cheddar cheese, grated
1   (16 ounce) jar taco sauce
1   (4 ounce) can green chilies
1   cup low fat sour cream
3   tablespoons chicken broth
1   large onion, diced

Brown diced onion in chicken broth. Add cooked ground turkey. Stir refried beans into turkey mixture. Spread into a 9x13-inch casserole sprayed with nonfat cooking spray. Sprinkle green chilies over top of turkey mixture. Spread half of cheese over mixture. Pour taco sauce over cheese. Sprinkle remaining cheese on top. Bake at 400 degrees, cool slightly. Spoon sour cream to make a cross on top of the casserole. Serve with tortilla chips.

# Easy Dip for Raw Vegetables

⅔   cup mayonnaise-type salad dressing
⅔   cup sour cream
1   tablespoon dried onion flakes
1   tablespoon parsley flakes
1   teaspoon seasoned salt
½   teaspoon Worcestershire sauce
2   drops hot pepper sauce
1   teaspoon dill weed

Mix all ingredients with mixer.

Serve with cauliflower, green peppers, green onions, carrots, celery or cherry tomatoes. Makes 1⅓ cups

# Hot Artichoke Spread

1   (14 ounce) can artichoke hearts, drained and chopped
1   cup mayonnaise
1   cup Parmesan cheese
⅛   teaspoon garlic powder

Mix all ingredients and put into ramekin.

Heat at 350 degrees for 20 minutes or until mixture bubbles.

Serve warm with crackers or chips.

# Spicy Black-Eyed Pea Dip

2    stalks celery, finely chopped

1    (8 ounce) can jalapeño peppers, chopped and seeded

¼    cup green bell pepper, fine chopped

1    large onion, peeled and finely chopped

1    teaspoon black pepper

2    tablespoons hot sauce

½    cup catsup

1    teaspoon salt

3    cubes chicken bouillon, crushed

¼    teaspoon nutmeg

¼    teaspoon cinnamon

3    (16 ounce) cans black-eyed peas

1    (14½ ounce) can tomatoes

2    cloves garlic, finely chopped

8    slices bacon, cooked

½    cup bacon grease

3    tablespoons flour

Combine celery, jalapeño pepper, bell pepper, onion, black pepper, hot sauce, catsup, salt, bouillon, nutmeg and cinnamon in a large pan. Bring to a slow simmer.

Slightly mash peas, being careful not to make a paste of them. Add peas to sauce. Repeat the gentle mashing procedure with the tomatoes. Add tomatoes and garlic to black-eyed pea mixture. Cook 30 minutes over moderate heat, stirring occasionally.

Cook bacon in a skillet, reserving ½ cup grease, and set bacon aside. Stir flour into the grease, mixing well to make a roux. Add roux to the black-eyed pea mixture.

Heat and stir for 10 minutes. Remove from heat, crumble bacon on top and stir. Serves 14 to 16

*This is best served hot, but is also popular cold. Freezes well.*


# Texas Crabgrass

⅓    cup butter

½    cup onion, finely chopped

1    (7½ ounce) can crabmeat, drained

½    cup Parmesan cheese

1    (10 ounce) package frozen chopped spinach, cooked and drained

Melt butter. Add onion and sauté until soft. Add crabmeat, cheese and spinach; heat through.

Serve hot with melba rounds or crackers.

# Basil Sun-Dried Tomato Spread

2   (8 ounce) packages of cream cheese
½   cup unsalted butter
2   cups fresh basil
1½  cups Romano cheese
2   cloves garlic
¼   cup olive oil
¼   cup pine nuts
5   ounces sun-dried tomatoes

Combine cream cheese and butter in food processor. Set aside.

Combine basil, parsley, Romano cheese and garlic in cleaned processor.

Add to the cheese mixture the olive oil and process.

Add pine nuts and pulse lightly. Set mixture aside.

Snip the sun dried tomatoes into strips or chunks. Cover with boiling water to soften. Drain.

Layer tomatoes and cheese mixtures in plastic wrap-lined bowl or spring form pan starting with the cream cheese mixture, then the cheese mixture, and then the tomato mixture. Repeat layers twice.

Chill several hours or overnight. Invert onto serving plate and garnish with fresh basil.

Serve with crackers.

# Mushroom Pâté

¾   pound fresh mushrooms, chopped
2   tablespoons butter
1   (8 ounce) package cream cheese
¾   teaspoon garlic salt

Sauté mushrooms in butter 5 to 10 minutes or until tender and liquid has evaporated.

Place in blender or food processor with cream cheese and garlic salt. Process until smooth.

Pack in a mold. Refrigerate at least three hours before serving.

Best if made day before serving. Serve with crackers.

# Seafood Supreme Spread

2 (8 ounce) packages cream cheese, softened
1 (8 ounce) package crabmeat flakes
2 tablespoons onion, finely chopped
1 tablespoon prepared horseradish
1 teaspoon Worcestershire sauce
4-5 drops hot pepper sauce
¼ cup chopped walnuts
paprika

Beat cream cheese one or two minutes with electric mixer until creamy.

Blend in remaining ingredients except walnuts and paprika.

Spread mixture in 9-inch pie plate.

Top with walnuts and sprinkle with paprika.

Bake uncovered at 375 degrees for 20 minutes or until golden brown.

# Party Crab Mold

2 (1 ounce) envelopes unflavored gelatin
½ cup cold water
½ cup boiling water
3 (8 ounce) packages cream cheese, softened
¾ cup lemon juice
1 teaspoon salt
1 teaspoon Worcestershire sauce
½ teaspoon hot pepper sauce
½ teaspoon grated onion
4 (6 ounce) cans lump crabmeat, drained
pimiento-stuffed green olives, sliced for garnish
fresh parsley, chopped for garnish

Lightly oil a 5½-cup mold.

Sprinkle gelatin over cold water, let stand 5 minutes. Add boiling water, stir until gelatin dissolves. Combine gelatin mixture with cream cheese, lemon juice, salt, Worcestershire sauce, hot pepper sauce and onion in a mixing bowl. Beat on medium speed of electric mixer until smooth. Stir in crabmeat. Pour into mold and chill until firm. Unmold and garnish with sliced olives and parsley. Serve with crackers.

# Harvest Time Pumpkin Dip

2   (8 ounce) packages cream cheese, softened
1   (16 ounce) package powdered sugar, sifted
1   (16 ounce) can pumpkin
2   teaspoons ground cinnamon
½   teaspoon ground nutmeg
    gingersnaps

Let cream cheese stand at room temperature until softened. In a large bowl, beat cream cheese at medium speed of an electric mixer until creamy.

Gradually add the powdered sugar, beating well.

Stir in pumpkin, cinnamon and nutmeg.

Serve immediately with gingersnaps for dipping, or cover and chill. Makes 5 cups

*Serve in a small pumpkin - either ceramic or fresh. Cut the top off a fresh pumpkin and remove the seeds and membrane.*

# Sherry Baked Brie

8   tablespoons butter
1   cup slivered almonds
1   cup golden raisins
8   tablespoons brown sugar
8   tablespoons dry sherry
1   (2 pound) wheel of Brie, trimmed of rind

Place butter in saucepan and melt. Stir in almonds, toss to coat with butter. Heat until nuts are brown.

Stir in raisins, brown sugar and sherry. Heat through.

Place Brie in serving dish. Spoon nuts over mixture. Heat oven to 350 degrees. Heat until Brie is bubbly, approximately 20-30 minutes.

Serve with sliced sour dough flute or other bread.

# Shrimp Mousse

| | |
|---|---|
| 1 | (10¾ ounce) can condensed tomato soup |
| 1 | (8 ounce) package cream cheese |
| 2 | envelopes unflavored gelatin |
| ½ | cup cold water |
| 1 | pound cooked bay shrimp, minced |
| ¼ | cup grated onion |
| 1 | cup celery, finely chopped |
| 1 | cup mayonnaise |
| 1 | teaspoon fresh lemon juice |
| | pinch of salt |
| | parsley, watercress, lemon slices for garnish |
| | assorted crackers |

Heat tomato soup and cream cheese in a double boiler over simmering water. Gently stir with wire whisk to blend.

In small bowl, dissolve gelatin in cold water. When hot mixture is completely blended, add dissolved gelatin, stirring to blend. Cool mixture to room temperature. When completely cool, add shrimp, onion, celery, mayonnaise, lemon juice and salt. Blend thoroughly and pour into a 5-cup decorative mold.

Chill in refrigerator at least four hours. When ready to serve, unmold on chilled serving platter, surround with parsley, watercress and lemon slices for garnish.

A separate plate or basket should be filled with an assortment of crackers for spreading. Serves 15-20

*May be prepared ahead, does not freeze well.*
*Use low fat or non-fat cream cheese and mayonnaise, and substitute crabmeat for shrimp.*

# Sausage Cheese Balls

| | |
|---|---|
| 1 | pound ground sausage (uncooked) |
| 1 | pound cheese, grated |
| 2 | cups dry biscuit mix |

Before mixing together have sausage and cheese at room temperature. Mix sausage and cheese, and knead. Add biscuit mix and mix well with hands. Make into walnut-sized balls and place on baking sheet.

Bake at 350 degrees 25-30 minutes. Drain on paper towels.

# Chicken Liver Pâté with Port Wine Aspic

2 teaspoons unflavored gelatin
1 cup port, divided
2 tablespoons sugar
1 tablespoon water
3 tablespoons red wine vinegar
½ teaspoon dry tarragon, crumbled
1 pound chicken or duck livers
1 cup milk
¼ cup cognac
1¼ cups butter, room temperature
1 cup onions, sliced
1 small green apple, peeled, cored, and sliced
¼ cup sherry
¼ cup whipping cream
1¼ teaspoons salt
1 teaspoon lemon juice

Aspic: Generously butter 8x4-inch loaf pan and set aside.

Dissolve gelatin in small bowl with ¼ cup port. Meanwhile, combine sugar and water in medium saucepan over medium high heat, stirring until dissolved. Cook until mixture is dark caramel color, about 8 to 10 minutes. Whisk in vinegar, remaining port and tarragon. Reduce heat and simmer about 2 minutes. Add gelatin, stirring until dissolved. Strain aspic through cheesecloth-lined colander into prepared loaf pan, covering ⅛ to ¼-inch of bottom. Chill until set.

Pâté: Combine the chicken or duck livers, milk, and cognac in medium bowl and soak 1 hour.

Melt ½ cup butter in large skillet over medium heat. Add onion and sauté until browned. Add apple and cook until soft, about 3 to 4 minutes.

Transfer mixture to processor or blender using a slotted spoon.

Drain livers. Return skillet to medium-high heat. Add livers and sauté until just pink, about 10-12 minutes. Add to onion mixture in processor or blender and blend until smooth.

Reduce heat under skillet to medium, add sherry to skillet and cook, stirring up any browned bits clinging to bottom of the pan.

*(continued on next page)*

48

*(Chicken Liver Pâté continued)*

Add pan juices and ¼ cup cream to liver mixture in processor and puree until smooth. Let stand until lukewarm.

Beat remaining butter in medium bowl until creamy. With machine running, gradually blend butter into liver mixture. Mix in salt and lemon juice.

Pour over chilled aspic, smoothing top. Refrigerate.

To serve, run sharp knife around edge of mold, dip mold briefly into hot water and invert pâté onto platter.

# Hot Mushroom and Clam Dip

| | |
|---|---|
| 1 | pound mushrooms, sliced |
| 2 | tablespoons butter |
| 1 | (8 ounce) package cream cheese |
| 1 | (16 ounce) container sour cream |
| 2 | (6½ ounce) cans minced clams, drained |
| 1 | tablespoon soy sauce |
| ¼ | teaspoon freshly ground black pepper |
| ½ | teaspoon seasoned salt |

Sauté mushrooms in butter until tender. In double boiler, melt cream cheese and sour cream, blending well. Add mushrooms, clams, soy sauce, pepper and seasoned salt. Place in chafing dish and serve with Homemade Melba Toast. Makes 4 cups

Homemade Melba Toast
  butter
  very thin slices white bread, crusts trimmed

Butter bread slices and cut into quarters. Bake at 250 degrees until crisp. These store well in airtight tins and may be done well in advance.

*Adorn this hot dip with fluted mushrooms dipped in lemon juice to prevent discoloration.*

# Artichoke Nibbles

2   (6 ounce) jars marinated artichoke hearts
1   small onion, chopped
1   clove garlic, minced
4   eggs, beaten
¼   cup fine bread crumbs
¼   teaspoon salt
⅛   teaspoon pepper
⅛   teaspoon hot pepper sauce
2   cups shredded cheddar cheese
2   tablespoons fresh parsley, minced

Preheat oven to 325 degrees. Grease a 9-inch square pan. Drain the marinade from one jar of the artichoke hearts into a small skillet and sauté the onion and garlic for five minutes or until the onion is transparent. Set aside.

Drain the other jar of artichokes, discarding marinade and chop all the artichokes finely.

Mix the eggs, crumbs and seasonings. Stir in the artichokes, cheese, parsley and onion mixture. Blend well.

Pour into prepared pan and bake for 30 minutes or until the center is firm to the touch. Remove from the oven and let sit for 15 minutes. Cut into 1-inch squares and serve warm or at room temperature.

# Herb Cucumber Sandwiches

24   slices white or wheat bread
1    (8 ounce) package cream cheese
2    English cucumbers, finely chopped
3½   ounces chopped fresh chives
2    tablespoons unsalted butter
½    ounce chopped pimientos

Mix softened cream cheese, butter with a mixer until creamy. Stir in cucumbers, chives and pimientos. Set aside. Using cookie or biscuit cutter cut out bread into desired design. Spread cream cheese on bread and make a sandwich. Can be made an hour before serving, but be sure to cover with plastic wrap to keep bread soft. Serves 12

# Cinnamon Walnuts

1½  cups sugar
½  cup water
½  teaspoon cinnamon
⅛  teaspoon cream of tartar
1  teaspoon vanilla
2½  cups of walnut halves

Boil first four ingredients until a little dropped in cold water forms soft ball (235 degree-soft ball stage on candy thermometer). Add 2½ cups walnuts, stir until coated, and cool. Add vanilla and stir. Pour out on wax paper. Separate with fork and enjoy.

*One of our members originally obtained this recipe in California in 1955. She has made it every Christmas since then.*

# Savory Southern Pecans

½  cup unsalted butter
1½  teaspoons ground cumin
¼  teaspoon ground red pepper
3  cups pecan halves
2  tablespoons sugar
1  teaspoon salt

Melt butter in a large saucepan and then add cumin and red pepper. Cook one minute.

Remove from heat; add pecans, sugar and salt, stirring to coat.

Spread pecans in a single layer in a 15x10x1-inch jelly-roll pan.

Bake at 300 degrees for 20 minutes, stirring occasionally.

Serve warm or at room temperature. Store in an airtight container up to five days. Makes 3 cups

# Chili Popcorn

| | |
|---|---|
| 3 | tablespoons melted butter |
| 1½ | teaspoons chili powder |
| ½ | teaspoon garlic powder |
| ½ | teaspoon paprika |
| 12 | cups popped popcorn |

Combine first four ingredients, drizzle over warm popcorn, stirring to coat. Makes 5 quarts

# Carmel Corn

| | |
|---|---|
| 7 | quarts popped corn |
| 1 | cup peanuts or other nuts |
| 2 | cups brown sugar |
| 2 | sticks butter |
| ½ | cup white corn syrup |
| 1 | teaspoon salt |
| 1 | teaspoon vanilla |
| ½ | teaspoon soda |

Combine all ingredients except soda and vanilla, bring to a boil.

Add soda and vanilla. Pour over corn and peanuts, mix well.

Place in greased roaster. Bake at 225 degrees for one hour, stirring every 15 minutes. Cool and break apart. Store in tightly covered container.

# Party Fruit Punch

| | |
|---|---|
| 2 | cups fruit punch liquid concentrate |
| 1 | (2 liter) bottle carbonated lemon-lime drink |
| 1 | (12 ounce) bag mixed berries frozen fruit |

Fruit ring: Place frozen berries in a bundt pan or ring jello mold. Add enough water to cover fruit. Put in freezer until frozen solid.

Mix together the fruit punch and lemon-lime drink in a punch bowl. Add fruit ring and serve.

# Tampico Fizz

¾ quart Tampico Punch orange drink
15 fresh mint twigs
½ cup lemon juice
1 cup boiling water
1 cup red currant jelly
½ cup cold water
1 (32 ounce) bottle ginger ale
ice

In a bowl, mash 12 of the mint twigs. Add the lemon juice, the boiling water, and the red currant jelly. When the jelly is dissolved, add the cold water.

Let it cool and then strain it into a punch bowl. Add Tampico, ice, and ginger ale. Garnish with remaining mint.

# Tampico Delight

1 quart Tampico Punch orange drink
1 quart grape juice
1 quart pineapple juice
chipped ice

Mix all the ingredients. Serve cold.

# Coffee Punch

2 quarts strong coffee
¾ cup sugar
½ pint heavy cream, whipped
1 cup chocolate syrup
1 quart vanilla ice cream

Combine coffee and sugar, cool. Freeze a portion in a 5-quart bundt pan or ring mold for ice ring. Refrigerate remainder. Before serving, mix coffee, cream, syrup, and ice cream which has been cut into chunks. Stir and put in punch bowl. Add ice ring.

# Cranberry Sparkle Punch

2 quarts cranberry juice, 2 cups reserved for ring mold
1 quart orange juice, chilled, 2 cups reserved for ring mold
2 quarts carbonated lemon-lime drink
1 (8 ounce) package whole frozen strawberries
vodka (optional)

Ice ring: Mix 2 cups cranberry juice and 2 cups orange juice. Place frozen strawberries in a 5-cup ring mold. Pour juice mixture over strawberries to near top of mold. Freeze.

Mix cranberry and orange juice in a punch bowl. When ready to serve, add lemon-lime drink and vodka to juices. Float ice ring in the punch bowl. Extra strawberries may be added to the bowl.

# Fruited Tea Punch

½ cup loose tea
1½ cups sugar
3 quarts water
1 (12 ounce) can frozen lemonade
4 sprigs fresh mint
1½ cups pineapple juice
1 (8 ounce) can of orange juice
2 quarts ginger ale

Make a strong tea from tea leaves and water. Steep with the mint leaves for 10 minutes. Remove mint and add sugar. Stir well. Add pineapple and orange juices and chill.

When ready to serve, add chilled ginger ale. Garnish each glass with a mint sprig and lime slice. Makes 1 gallon

# Le Jazz Hot

4 ounces light red wine
½ ounce cinnamon schnapps
1 thin strip of orange zest
1 cinnamon stick

Pour the red wine over ice in a tall glass. Pour the schnapps on top of wine without stirring. Garnish with the orange zest and the cinnamon stick. Makes 1 drink

# Amaretto Crème

| | | |
|---|---|---|
| 1 | cup half and half | |
| 1 | (14 ounce) can sweetened condensed milk | |
| 1½ | cups Amaretto | |
| 1 | teaspoon instant coffee granules | |
| 2 | tablespoons chocolate syrup | |
| 1 | teaspoon vanilla extract | |

Combine all ingredients in blender for 30 seconds.

Mixture may be bottled in tightly sealed container and refrigerated for two months. Shake before serving.

*May use whiskey or rum instead of Amaretto.*

*Makes a wonderful gift in a colored bottle with a long cork in the top.*

# Egg Nog Supreme

| | |
|---|---|
| 12 | eggs, divided |
| 1 | cup granulated sugar |
| 13 | ounces brandy |
| 26 | ounces rye or rum |
| 2 | cups light cream |

Beat 12 egg yolks with sugar until lemon colored and thick; then add slowly the brandy, rye or rum, and light cream. Beat to blend well and chill one hour or overnight to allow egg to mellow.

Before serving, put egg yolk mixture in punch bowl. In separate bowl, beat 12 egg whites until stiff. Set aside.

In another bowl beat 3 cups whipping cream until stiff. Fold in egg whites and then add to egg yolk mixture in punch bowl. Sprinkle with grated nutmeg.

# Wassail

| | |
|---|---|
| ½ | gallon apple cider |
| ¼ | cup brown sugar |
| 3 | ounces lemon concentrate |
| 3 | ounces orange concentrate |
| ½ | tablespoon whole cloves |
| ½ | teaspoon allspice |
| ½ | teaspoon ground nutmeg |
| 3 | cinnamon sticks |
| 1 | cup rum (optional) |

Combine cider, sugar and concentrates. Place spices in cheesecloth square, tie the corners and place in the cider mixture. Simmer for 20 minutes and serve hot. Before serving, add rum if desired.

*This makes a festive holiday party drink.*

# Hot Buttered Rum Batter

| | |
|---|---|
| 1 | pound unsalted butter (not margarine) |
| 1½ | cups bark brown sugar |
| 1½ | cups super fine granulated sugar |
| 1 | quart good quality vanilla ice cream, softened |
| ½ | teaspoon cinnamon |
| ½ | teaspoon nutmeg |
| ½ | teaspoon cloves |

In a medium saucepan or microwave safe dish, melt butter. Place sugars and spices in a large mixing bowl; add melted butter and beat on low speed with an electric mixer until blended and smooth. Add soft, softened ice cream and mix very well.

Store covered in the refrigerator. Keeps well for several weeks.

To serve, add a generous tablespoon of batter, 1 jigger of dark rum to a mug. Mix. Fill mug with boiling water and stir. Makes batter for 60 to 80 servings.

*Instead of super fine granulated sugar, you may use 2 cups regular granulated sugar processed in a food processor or blender for three minutes.*

# Heatherbed Alm Doodler

20 cups apple cider
12 cups rose, burgundy or Chianti wine
6-8 cinnamon sticks
2 teaspoons whole cloves
2 cups sugar

Put spices in cheesecloth. Combine cider, wine, spices, and sugar. Heat to just below boiling. Allow to steep for 1 hour. This is best made a day ahead and reheated to serve.

# Sneaky Pete Punch

1 cup powdered sugar
2 cups cranberry juice
2 (6 ounce) cans frozen orange juice, slightly thawed
2 (6 ounce) cans frozen lemonade, slightly thawed
48 ounces carbonated lemon-lime drink
1 Fifth vodka

Using a whisk, add sugar to cranberry juice and stir well until completely dissolved. Stir in remaining ingredients. Pour into individual glasses and freeze until slushy. Serve frozen. Serves 16-20

# Vodka Slush

1 (46 ounce) can pineapple juice
1 (12 ounce) can frozen lemonade
1 (12 ounce) can frozen orange juice
1 quart ginger ale
2 cups vodka

Mix together pineapple and orange juices and lemonade. Pour into container and freeze. When ready to serve, fill glass half way with mix and fill with carbonated lemon-lime drink.

*The mix and lemon-lime drink may be combined and served in either a pitcher or punch bowl.*

# Cappuccino

2 cups very strong coffee
2 cups milk
1 tablespoon sugar
1 tablespoon cocoa
1 ounce brandy
1 ounce dark crème de
   cocoa
  whipped cream
  cinnamon sticks

Mix coffee, milk, sugar, and cocoa in a saucepan and bring to a boil. Remove from heat. Add brandy and crème de cocoa. Pour immediately into demitasse cups or coffee cups. Garnish with a large dollop of whipped cream and place a cinnamon stick in each cup for a swizzle stick. Serves 4


# Mocha Punch

2 quarts strong coffee
¾ cup sugar
½ pint cream, whipped
1 cup chocolate syrup
1 quart vanilla ice cream

Mix coffee and sugar. Pour enough in a 5-cup ring mold to almost fill; freeze. Just before serving, in a punch bowl mix remaining coffee and sugar mixture with whipped cream and chocolate syrup. Add ice cream a scoop at a time and stir. Add iced coffee ring and serve.

# Breakfasts
# and
# Brunches

# Garlic Cheese Grits

1   cup grits
1   roll garlic cheese
½   stick margarine
2   eggs
¼   cup milk
    cayenne pepper to taste
    salt (optional)

Topping
¼   cup grated cheddar cheese
    paprika

Cook 1 cup grits with 3 cups water. Add garlic cheese, margarine, eggs, milk, pepper. Pour into greased baking dish. Sprinkle cheddar cheese and paprika on top. Bake at 300 degrees for 45 minutes.

# Shrimp 'N' Grits

2-3 slices of thick-sliced
    bacon
1   small-medium sweet
    onion, chopped
1   pound medium raw
    shrimp, peeled and
    deveined
    grits (not instant) cooked
    according to package
    directions for 3-6
    servings
    orange slices

Sauce
1   heaping tablespoon flour
¼   teaspoon instant coffee in
    ½ cup hot water

Chop bacon and fry until crisp. Remove. Sauté onion in bacon drippings until translucent.

Add shrimp and toss until pink. (Don't overcook).

Remove shrimp with slotted spoon and add sauce mixture to skillet. Stir constantly until thickened. (about two minutes.) Return shrimp and bacon to pan and heat thoroughly. Serve over spoonful of hot grits. Garnish with an orange slice. Serves 4-6

*This is a good brunch dish served with curried fruit and hot biscuits (and mimosas, of course). May use milk in place of water for creamier grits.*

60

*Photo on right ~*
Luscious Lemon Bread, page 84
and Strawberry Bread, page 81

# Italian Scrambled Eggs

2 tablespoons butter
1¼ cups sliced mushrooms
¼ pound prosciutto or ham, diced
¾ teaspoon minced garlic
½ medium green bell pepper, diced
½ pound asparagus, trimmed and cut into 1-inch lengths
10 eggs
1½ tablespoons minced fresh basil or 1 teaspoon dried basil
1 teaspoon ground oregano
¼ teaspoon salt
¾ teaspoon freshly ground black pepper
¾ teaspoon crushed red pepper flakes
6 ounces cream cheese, softened
1½ cups shredded mozzarella cheese
⅓ cup freshly grated Parmesan cheese
4 tablespoons butter

In a large skillet, heat 2 tablespoons butter; add mushrooms, prosciutto, garlic and green pepper. Sauté over medium heat until vegetables are tender. Remove with a slotted spoon and set aside.

Blanch asparagus in boiling salted water for 1-2 minutes until crisp-tender. Drain well and set aside. Whisk together eggs, herbs and seasonings. Cut cream cheese into small cubes and add to egg mixture.

Heat remaining 4 tablespoons butter in skillet. Add egg mixture. Cook over medium heat while folding mixture with a spatula to blend in cream cheese. When eggs are half set, add warm vegetable-prosciutto mixture, mozzarella, Parmesan and warm asparagus. Continue to cook while gently folding in cheeses with a spatula. When eggs are just done, serve immediately. Serves 6

*Broccoli can be substituted for asparagus.*

*Photo on left ~*
Ribbons, Linens and
Lingerie, page 20

# Tortilla Egg Scramble

| | |
|---|---|
| 1 | pound bacon |
| 1 | large onion, chopped |
| 1 | green pepper, chopped |
| 6 | corn tortillas, cut in thin strips |
| 10 | eggs, stirred for scrambling |
| ½ | cup cheddar cheese, shredded |
| ½ | teaspoon salt |
| ¼ | teaspoon pepper |

In a 10-inch uncovered skillet, fry bacon crisp. Crumble the bacon and set aside.

Stir-fry onions and pepper in bacon drippings and set aside.

Fry tortilla strips in drippings. Discard bacon drippings and return bacon, vegetables and tortilla strips to pan. Scramble eggs with this mixture. Cook for about 15 minutes.

To serve, use a large bowl and sprinkle cheese over the top. Serve immediately with toast and jelly and picante. Serves 4-6

*You may use liquid egg product instead of real eggs, fry the vegetables and tortilla strips in oil, and use precooked bacon if you wish.*

# Farmer's Casserole

| | |
|---|---|
| 3 | cups frozen shredded hash brown potatoes |
| ¾ | cup shredded Monterey Jack cheese with jalapeño peppers or 3 ounces shredded cheddar cheese |
| 1 | cup diced fully cooked ham or Canadian-style bacon |
| ¼ | cup sliced green onions |
| 4 | beaten eggs |
| 1 | (12 ounce) can evaporated milk |
| ¼ | teaspoon pepper |
| ⅛ | teaspoon salt |

Grease a 2-quart square baking dish. Arrange the potatoes evenly in the bottom of the dish. Sprinkle with cheese, ham, and green onions.

In a medium mixing bowl combine eggs, milk, pepper and salt. Pour the egg mixture over potato, cheese, ham mixture. Bake uncovered for 45 minutes at 350 degrees or until center appears set. Let stand 5 minutes before serving. Serves 6

# Egg and Green Chili Casserole

8 ounces Monterey Jack cheese, shredded
8 ounces cheddar cheese, shredded
2 (4 ounce) cans chopped green chilies, drained
1 bunch green onions, chopped
5 eggs
7 egg whites
3 tablespoons nonfat plain yogurt
1 tomato, thinly sliced

Coat a 3 quart or 13x9x2-inch glass baking dish with non-stick cooking spray. Combine cheeses, green chilies, and green onions; spread on bottom of dish. Beat eggs and egg whites together with yogurt. Pour over cheeses, making a space with fork so eggs will go through to bottom. Refrigerate overnight.

Place in cold oven, and bake at 350 degrees for 15 minutes.

Add sliced tomatoes along top of casserole and continue baking for 15-20 minutes longer, or until done. Serve hot. Serves 12

*Reduced fat cheeses can be used.*

# Sour Cream Coffee Cake

½ cup sugar
4 teaspoons cinnamon
½ cup chopped walnuts
1 stick butter or margarine
1 cup sugar
2 eggs
1 cup sour cream
2 cups flour
1 teaspoon baking powder
1 teaspoon vanilla
1 teaspoon baking soda, (heaping)

Grease and flour tube pan. Mix topping of ½ cup sugar, cinnamon and walnuts. Set aside.

Combine and beat 1 cup of sugar, eggs, and sour cream in mixer. Combine flour, baking powder, and soda and stir into batter. Add vanilla.

Swirl topping into the batter. It will look very dark brown. Bake at 350 degrees for 50 minutes. Let sit for 5 minutes and turn onto a plate.

# Oatmeal Pancakes

| | |
|---|---|
| 1 | cup flour |
| 1 | tablespoon sugar |
| 1 | teaspoon baking soda |
| ½ | teaspoon salt |
| ½ | teaspoon cinnamon |
| 1¼ | cups oatmeal (old fashioned) |
| 2 | cups buttermilk |
| 2 | eggs slightly beaten |
| 4 | tablespoons butter or margarine, melted |
| 1-1½ | cups fresh small blueberries (optional) |
| 1 | ripe banana, mashed (optional) |

Mix dry ingredients together in large bowl. In separate bowl add buttermilk to oatmeal, then eggs and mix well. Add oatmeal mixture to dry ingredients, mix. Add melted butter and mix just until well blended. (Do not overmix).

If using blueberries or other optional ingredients, carefully fold in.

Heat griddle or frying pan until hot, add enough oil to prevent sticking. When water droplets sprinkled on surface bounce, surface is ready. This is a dense batter so finished pancake will be very moist. Only turn once.

# Breakfast Take Alongs

| | |
|---|---|
| ⅔ | cup butter or margarine |
| ⅔ | cup sugar |
| 1 | egg |
| 1 | teaspoon vanilla |
| ¾ | cup all purpose flour |
| ½ | teaspoon soda |
| ½ | teaspoon salt |
| 1½ | cups uncooked oats (quick or old fashioned) |
| 1 | cup (4 ounces) shredded cheddar cheese |
| ½ | cup wheat germ or fine chopped nuts |
| 6 | slices crispy cooked bacon, crumbled |

Beat together butter, sugar, egg and vanilla until well blended.

Add combined flour, soda and salt; mix well. Stir in oats, cheese, wheat germ and bacon.

Drop by rounded tablespoonfuls onto greased cookie sheet. Bake in preheated oven at 350 degrees for 12-14 minutes or until edges are golden brown.

Cool 1 minute on cookie sheet; remove to wire cooling rack. Store in loosely covered container in refrigerator or at room temperature. Makes 3 dozen

# Mushroom Crust Quiche

3 tablespoons butter
½ pound mushrooms, coarsely chopped
½ cup finely crushed saltine crackers
2 tablespoons butter
¾ cup finely chopped green onions
2 cups shredded Swiss cheese
1 cup cottage cheese
3 eggs
¼ teaspoon ground cayenne
¼ teaspoon paprika

In skillet, melt 3 tablespoons butter over medium heat; add mushrooms and cook until limp. Stir in crushed crackers.

Turn mixture into well-greased 9-inch pie pan, pressing mixture evenly over pan bottom and up sides.

In same skillet, melt remaining 2 tablespoons butter over medium heat; add onion and cook until transparent.

Spread onions over mushroom crust, then sprinkle evenly with shredded cheese.

In food processor, whirl cottage cheese, eggs and cayenne pepper until smooth. Pour mixture into crust and sprinkle with paprika.

Bake at 350 degrees for 20-25 minutes or until knife inserted just off center comes out clean. Let stand for 10-15 minutes before serving. Serves 4-6

*Low fat cheeses can be used.*

# Apple Cinnamon French Toast

| | | |
|---|---|---|
| 1 | large loaf French bread |
| 8 | extra large eggs |
| 3½ | cups milk |
| 1 | cup sugar |
| 1 | tablespoon vanilla |
| 3 | teaspoons cinnamon |
| 1 | teaspoon nutmeg |
| 6-8 | medium sized cooking apples (Cortland, Macintosh) |
| ⅛ | of 1 stick of butter |

Slice bread into 1½ inch slices. Spray 9x13-inch glass pan with corn oil or non-stick spray. Arrange bread in glass dish, placing tightly together.

In separate bowl, beat together eggs, ½ cup sugar, milk and vanilla (by hand, with whisk, for about 30 seconds. Pour one half of egg/milk mixture over bread.

Peel, core and slice apples. Place sliced apples on top of bread to cover. Pour balance of egg/milk mixture evenly over apples.

Mix remaining ½ cup sugar with cinnamon and nutmeg and sprinkle evenly over top of apples.

Dot with butter. Cover and refrigerate overnight.

Next day: Preheat oven to 350 degrees. Uncover dish and bake in oven 1 hour. It will rise high and brown nicely. Remove from oven and allow to rest for 5-10 minutes before serving.

Cut into squares and serve with heated syrup, plus smoked sausage, bacon or your favorite breakfast meat. Serves 10-12

# Grand Marnier French Toast

| | |
|---|---|
| 1 | (1-pound) loaf unsliced white bread |
| 4 | eggs |
| 1 | cup milk |
| 2 | tablespoons Grand Marnier liqueur |
| 1 | tablespoon sugar |
| ½ | teaspoon pure vanilla extract |
| ¼ | teaspoon salt |
| ¼ | teaspoon freshly grated orange peel |
| | vegetable oil |
| 3 | tablespoons butter, melted |
| | powdered sugar |
| 1 | orange, thinly sliced (optional) |

Slice bread into eight ¾-inch slices. In medium bowl, beat eggs with milk, Grand Marnier, sugar, vanilla, salt and orange peel until well blended.

Dip each piece of bread into liquid mixture until well saturated. Place in a flat baking dish. Pour remaining liquid over bread. Cover and refrigerate overnight.

In skillet, heat oil and sauté bread until golden on both sides.

Brush with butter and sprinkle with powdered sugar. Top with orange slice and serve immediately with maple syrup. Serves 4.

# Mock Cheese Blintzes

| | |
|---|---|
| 12 | ounces cream cheese, softened |
| ½ | cup sugar |
| 1 | teaspoon pure vanilla extract |
| 1 | egg |
| 2 | loaves white sandwich bread |
| ¾ | cup butter, melted |
| ¾ | cup sugar |
| 2 | teaspoons ground cinnamon |

In medium bowl, beat together cream cheese, sugar, vanilla and egg; set aside.

Trim crusts off bread. Using a rolling pin, roll each slice until flat. Keep flattened slices under damp towel to prevent drying.

Spread cream cheese mixture on rolled bread slices. Roll up each slice like a jelly roll. Cut each roll in half. At this point, rollups may be frozen.

Dip each roll in melted butter, then in mixture of sugar and cinnamon.

Bake at 400 degrees for 15 minutes. Serve immediately. Makes 78 2-inch rolls

# Hot Ham Happy Sandwiches

| | |
|---|---|
| 14 | sandwich rolls |
| 2 | sticks margarine or butter |
| 3 | tablespoons mustard |
| ½ | teaspoon poppy seeds (optional) |
| 1 | tablespoon Worcestershire sauce |
| 1 | medium onion, chopped |
| 14 | slices ham, thinly sliced or shaved |
| 14 | slices Swiss cheese |
| | aluminum foil |

Combine margarine, mustard, poppy seeds, Worcestershire sauce, onion and blend well.

Spread on both sides of rolls.

Place ham, cheese in roll.

Wrap individually in aluminum foil; can be refrigerated or frozen at this point.

Bake for 15 minutes at 400 degrees. Serve immediately. Serves 14

# Eggs Portugal

| | |
|---|---|
| 8 | slices white bread |
| ¾ | pound sharp cheddar cheese, grated |
| 1½ | pounds skinless sausages |
| 2½ | cups milk |
| 4 | eggs |
| | pinch salt |
| 1 | cup mushrooms, canned or fresh |
| ½ | cup dry vermouth, or white wine |

In an 8x14-inch casserole dish place 8 slices cubed bread with crusts trimmed off. Sprinkle grated cheddar cheese over the bread cubes.

Fry sausage and cut into thirds. Spread over the bread/cheese mixture.

Mix the milk and eggs together, with a pinch of salt, if desired. Pour over the bread, cheese, and sausage. Add mushrooms and ½ cup vermouth or wine. Bake 1-1½ hours at 300 degrees.

Scoop and serve with champagne and sweet rolls. Serves 8

*Can be stored overnight in the refrigerator for baking the next morning.*

# Pineapple Delight Sandwiches

1    (8 ounce) package cream cheese, softened
1    small can crushed pineapple, well drained
⅛    teaspoon almond extract
6-8  maraschino cherries, drained
4-6  drops red food coloring
1    loaf bread, white, wheat, or your favorite
1    tube red decorating cake gel
1    tube green decorating cake gel
1    tube brown decorating cake gel
1    tube yellow decorating cake gel

Let cream cheese remain at room temperature to soften. Mix until creamy.

Place pineapple between paper towels to remove excess moisture. This is an important step to avoid sandwiches becoming soggy. Press out excess juice and discard paper towels.

Add pineapple to cream cheese and blend well.

Add extract.

Divide cream cheese pineapple mixture in half. In one half add the cherries and red food coloring.

Using party turnover press (available at specialty shops) trim crusts from bread and fill sandwiches with mixture and fold over and press. For the half filled with pink mixture decorate as watermelon using green for rind, red for center and brown for seeds.

Paint sandwiches with paint brush. Allow to air dry for 20 minutes (not longer or sandwich with dry out).

For second half of mixture, paint with yellow for lemon and green for rind.

*Kids are not the only ones who enjoy these fun sandwiches made to look like watermelon and lemons. Great for a tea or special get together and always a great "conversation" food. Remember, if you're going to have a party - then have fun party food.*

69

# Roman Apple Cake

1½ cups all-purpose flour, sifted
½ cup brown sugar
½ cup white sugar
½ cup (1 stick) cold butter cut into bits
½ teaspoon cinnamon
⅛ teaspoon salt (omit if you used salted butter)
1 teaspoon soda
½ cup buttermilk or sour milk
1 egg
1 large or 2 small tart apples

To the sifted flour add brown sugar, white sugar, butter bits, cinnamon, salt. Use your hands to crumble this mixture until blended, but not oily. Divide the crumbs into 2 parts.

Stir into ½ of the crumbs the beaten egg, soda and buttermilk and arrange this batter in a deep greased oven-proof 9-inch pie plate.

Place the pared, cored, and thinly sliced apples over the batter. Cover this with the remaining crumbs. You may dot the top with butter and cinnamon.

Bake the cake in a moderate oven 325 degrees for about 1 hour. Cake may be served with cream or whipped cream.

# Muffalata Spread

½ cup peperoncini peppers
½ cup cherry peppers
¼ cup black olives
¼ cup green olives
½ cup roasted red peppers
½ cup artichoke hearts
5 tablespoons capers
½ teaspoon chopped garlic
5 tablespoons chopped shallots
1 finely chopped anchovy
1-2 cups olive oil
hot pepper sauce

Chop first ten ingredients in food processor or by hand. Add olive oil and mix. Add hot pepper sauce to taste. Use as filling for sandwich rolls.

70

# Bacon, Onion and Tomato Frittata

½   pound bacon
1   tablespoon olive oil
1   medium sliced onion
2   medium peeled, seeded
      and chopped tomatoes
10  large eggs
⅓   cup chopped fresh basil
½   cup freshly grated Parme-
      san cheese
½   teaspoon salt
⅛   teaspoon pepper

In medium broiler proof nonstick skillet cook bacon until crisp. Using slotted spoon, transfer bacon to paper towels and drain. Pour off all but 1 tablespoon drippings.

Add olive oil to skillet. Add thinly sliced onion and cook over medium high heat until golden, stirring frequently. Cook about 5 minutes. Reduce heat to medium low.

Add tomatoes and cook until almost all liquid evaporates, stirring frequently. Cook about 10 minutes.

Preheat broiler.

Whisk eggs in large bowl until frothy. Whisk in basil and season with salt and pepper. Pour into skillet with vegetables.

Cook over medium heat until bottom is just golden and top is still unset, occasionally lifting edges of frittata and tilting pan to let uncooked egg run underneath. Cook about 10 minutes.

Sprinkle top with Parmesan cheese.

Broil frittata until top puffs and turns golden, about 3 minutes.

Slide frittata onto platter.

Serve warm or at room temperature, cutting into wedges.

*Can be made 2 hours ahead and covered.*

# Poppy Seed Dressing

1½ cups sugar
1 tablespoon dry mustard
2 teaspoons vinegar
1 tablespoon onion juice
3 cups oil
3 tablespoons poppy seeds

Mix the first 4 ingredients in the blender on high. Gradually add the oil. Mix in poppy seeds.

Serve over sliced bananas, pineapple chunks and sliced oranges. May be used as a dip on a fruit plate.

# Breads

# Blue Corn Muffins

| | | |
|---|---|---|
| 1 | stick unsalted butter | |
| 8 | tablespoons butter fla-vored shortening | |
| 4 | serrano chilies, seeded and minced | |
| 3 | cloves garlic, minced | |
| 1 | cup flour | |
| 1¼ | cups blue cornmeal or yellow cornmeal | |
| 2 | tablespoons sugar | |
| 1 | teaspoon baking powder | |
| 1½ | teaspoons salt | |
| 3 | eggs | |
| 1¼ | cups milk, at room temperature | |
| 3 | tablespoons chopped fresh cilantro | |
| | olive oil for brushing | |

Preheat oven to 400 degrees.

In small saucepan, gently melt butter and shortening over low heat. Add chilies and sauté for 10 minutes. Set aside.

In large mixing bowl, sift flour, cornmeal, sugar, baking powder, and salt. In another bowl, beat eggs slightly, add melted butter, shortening, chilies and garlic. Stir in milk. Pour wet ingredients into flour mixture. Mix until moistened and smooth. Add cilantro. Pour into greased or paper-lined muffin tins, or greased corn stick molds, to which you have added a few drops of olive oil. Bake 20-25 minutes, until cornbread is golden brown. Makes 8-10 muffins

# Breakfast Scones

| | |
|---|---|
| 2 | cups all-purpose flour |
| 1 | tablespoon baking powder |
| 2 | tablespoons sugar |
| ½ | teaspoon salt |
| ¼ | cup shortening |
| 2 | eggs |
| ⅓ | cup milk |

Sift flour, baking powder, sugar and salt into mixing bowl. Cut in short-ening until it resembles coarse meal.

Beat eggs, add milk and stir both into flour mixture with a fork. Do not overbeat. Turn out on a floured surface. Knead 5-6 times. Roll out ½ inch thick and cut with a 2-inch biscuit cutter. Place on a lightly greased griddle or skillet preheated to medium heat. Cook 10 minutes then turn and cook 10 minutes on the other side.

*May be dipped in sugar when removed from griddle. Currants may be added to dry ingredients before cutting in the shortening.*

74

# Herb Focaccia

3½ cups all-purpose flour, divided
1 teaspoon sugar
1 teaspoon salt
1 package fast acting yeast
1 cup water
5-6 tablespoons olive oil, divided
1 egg
1 teaspoons dried rosemary or basil leaves, crushed

Grease cookie sheet.

In large bowl, combine 1 cup flour, sugar, salt and yeast. Mix well.

In a small saucepan heat water and 2 tablespoons of oil until very warm (120-130 degrees). Add warm liquid and egg to flour mixture. Blend at low speed until moistened; beat 2 minutes at medium speed.

By hand stir in an additional 1¾ cups flour until dough pulls away from sides of bowl. On floured surface, knead in ¾ cup flour until dough is smooth and elastic, about 5 minutes. Place dough on greased cookie sheet. Roll or press to 12-inch circle. Cover loosely with greased plastic wrap and cloth towel. Let rise in warm place (80-85 degrees) until light and doubled in size, about 30 minutes.

Heat oven to 400 degrees. Uncover dough. With fingers, or handle of a wooden spoon, poke holes in dough at 1-inch intervals. Drizzle 3-4 teaspoons olive oil over top of dough. Sprinkle evenly with rosemary.

Bake at 400 degrees for 17 to 27 minutes or until golden brown. Immediately remove from cookie sheet; cool on wire rack.

# Currant Cream Scones

2 cups flour
2 teaspoons baking powder
2 tablespoons sugar, divided
½ teaspoon salt
6 tablespoons unsalted butter, cut into 10 pieces
¾ cups currants
2 large eggs, well beaten
½ cup plus 1 tablespoon heavy cream, divided

Preheat oven to 425 degrees.

Sift flour, baking powder, 1 tablespoon of the sugar and the salt into a mixing bowl. Add butter, working it into flour mixture with fingertips until mixture resembles cookie crumbs. Add currants and toss. Make a well in the flour mixture and add eggs and ½ of the cream. Mix with a wooden spoon until dough begins to clump together. The dough may be very sticky. Knead in the bowl for about 30 seconds; do not overwork dough. Turn dough out onto a lightly floured surface and halve. Form each half into a ball and flatten to form a circle about ¾ inch thick and 5 inches in diameter. Cut each circle into 8 wedges. Place wedges about 1 inch apart on a lightly buttered baking sheet. Brush tops with remaining cream and sprinkle with remaining sugar.

Bake 10-15 minutes, or until lightly browned. Serve warm with raspberry or black currant conserve.

*In place of currants use golden raisins, dried cherries or dried cranberries.*
*May be made ahead and reheated in 400 degree oven for 5 minutes. May be frozen right after baking. Scones are an essential part of traditional afternoon tea.*

# Herbed Bubble Bread

| | |
|---|---|
| 2 | loaves frozen bread dough |
| 2 | tablespoons Parmesan cheese |
| ½ | teaspoon dill weed |
| ¼ | teaspoon rosemary leaves, crushed |
| ¼ | cup margarine |
| 1 | teaspoon leaf thyme |
| ½ | teaspoon sweet basil, crushed |

Thaw frozen bread dough in refrigerator overnight. Allow to rise at room temperature for one hour. Knead both loaves of bread into one ball. Roll dough into a 12-inch square. Cut into 25 squares.

Melt margarine and add Parmesan cheese and herbs. Mix well. Dip each square of dough into herb mixture and place in greased bundt pan, overlapping each square slightly. Let rise in a warm place until doubled in size. Bake at 350 degrees for 30 to 40 minutes. Best served warm.

# Kiss Me Rolls

| | |
|---|---|
| 1 | cup sour cream |
| 1½ | packages dry yeast |
| ⅓ | cup warm water |
| 2 | sticks butter |
| 4 | cups flour, divided |
| ½ | cup sugar |
| 2 | eggs, well beaten |
| ½ | teaspoon salt |

Heat sour cream in a double boiler until slightly yellow around the edges. Soften yeast in warm water and let stand for 15 minutes. Place butter, sugar and salt in a large bowl. Add sour cream and stir until butter melts. Cool to lukewarm. Blend 1 cup flour into the sour cream mixture and beat until smooth. Stir in yeast until well mixed. Add second cup of flour and beat until smooth. Add beaten eggs. Add remaining 2 cups of flour, one at a time.

Cover and refrigerate at least 6 hours (overnight is best.) Roll out dough on a floured surface and cut into desired shapes. Brush with melted butter and let rise about 1 hour. Bake for 10-15 minutes or until golden brown.

# Rich Refrigerator Rolls

5-5½  cups all purpose flour
2  packages quick rise yeast
½  cup sugar
1  teaspoon salt
1  cup water
½  cup butter or margarine
3  eggs

In large mixer bowl, combine 2 cups flour, yeast, sugar and salt; mix well.

In saucepan heat water and butter until warm (120-130 degrees; butter does not need to melt). Add to flour mixture. Add eggs. Blend at low speed until moistened; beat 3 minutes at medium speed. By hand, gradually stir in enough remaining flour to make a soft dough. Cover with plastic wrap and foil. Refrigerate 6 to 12 hours.

While dough is chilling, punch down several times. Before baking shape into rolls as follows: Divide into 4 parts. Shape each fourth into the rolls of your choice (see note). Refrigerate remaining dough until ready to use. Place rolls in greased muffin pans or on greased cookie sheets, depending on the roll variety selected. Cover; let rise at room temperature until almost doubled, 10 to 15 minutes. Bake at 400 degrees, for the time specified, until golden brown. Remove from pans or cookie sheets. Serve warm or cold.

*A rich, golden, tender roll that's easy to make. No kneading required. From this one dough you can make four different kinds of rolls: cloverleaf, miniature rolls, Parker House or crescent. Directions are given for a mixture of all four kinds, but you can make any combination of varieties.*

*(continued on next page)*

78

Cloverleaf Rolls

¼ recipe Rich Refrigerator Rolls dough

Divide dough into 3 parts. Divide each third into 6 pieces. Shape each piece into a smooth ball. Place 3 balls in each greased muffin pan cup. Cover, let rise. Bake 8 to 10 minutes. Makes 6 rolls

Miniature Rolls

¼ recipe Rich Refrigerator Rolls dough

Divide dough into 3 parts. Divide each third into 4 pieces. Shape each piece into a smooth ball about the size of a walnut. Place one ball in each greased miniature muffin pan cup. Cover; let rise. Bake 8-10 minutes. Makes 10 rolls.

Parker House Rolls

¼ recipe Rich Refrigerator Rolls dough
1 tablespoon butter, melted

On lightly floured surface, roll dough into a 12x9-inch rectangle. Cut into 12 squares. Brush with butter. Make an off-center crease in each square. Fold so top half overlaps slightly. Press edges together. Place 2 to 3 inches apart on greased cookie sheets. Cover; let rise. Bake 6 to 8 minutes. Makes 12 rolls

Crescent Rolls

¼ recipe Rich Refrigerator Rolls dough
1 tablespoon butter, melted

On lightly floured surface roll dough to a ½-inch circle. Brush with butter. Cut into 10 wedges. Starting with wide end of wedge, roll toward point. Place point down, 2 to 3 inches apart, on greased cookie sheets. Curve to form a crescent shape. Cover, let rise. Bake 6 to 8 minutes. Makes 10 rolls

# Cinnamon Rolls

**Dough**

| | |
|---|---|
| 2 | packages yeast |
| ½ | cup sugar |
| 1 | cup lukewarm water |
| 1 | cup milk |
| 1 | cup shortening |
| 2 | teaspoons salt |
| 3 | eggs, well beaten |
| 6 | cups flour |

**Filling**

| | |
|---|---|
| 1 | stick margarine |
| 1 | cup sugar |
| 3 | teaspoons cinnamon |

**Frosting**

| | |
|---|---|
| 1 | can cream cheese frosting |

Dissolve yeast in water and sugar. Let stand 5 minutes. Heat milk, shortening, and salt until shortening is melted. Let cool.

Add milk mixture to yeast. Add eggs then add flour one cup at a time. Beat well, but do not knead. Refrigerate overnight.

Divide dough into two balls. Roll each piece on a floured board. Melt margarine and add sugar and cinnamon. Spread onto dough. Roll up, jelly roll fashion, and cut into one-inch slices.

Place on two cookie sheets. Let rise about 30 minutes. Bake at 400 degrees for 25-30 minutes. Cool slightly and ice with frosting. Makes 24 rolls

# Cheese Biscuits

| | |
|---|---|
| 2 | cups biscuit baking mix |
| ¾ | cup cold water |
| ¾ | cup grated sharp cheddar cheese |
| 1 | ounce butter or margarine, melted |
| 1 | teaspoon garlic salt, or to taste |
| 1 | tablespoon parsley flakes |
| ½ | teaspoon Italian seasoning |

Preheat oven to 450 degrees. Mix melted butter, garlic salt, parsley flakes and Italian seasoning. Set aside. Mix biscuit baking mix, water and cheese. Drop by large spoonfuls onto a greased baking sheet. Bake 8-10 minutes. After baking and while hot, brush on melted butter mixed with garlic salt, parsley flakes and the Italian seasoning.

# Angel Biscuits

| | |
|---|---|
| 1 | package yeast |
| 2 | tablespoons lukewarm water |
| 5 | cup unbleached flour |
| ¼ | cup sugar |
| 3 | teaspoons baking powder |
| 1 | teaspoon baking soda |
| 1 | teaspoon salt |
| 1 | cup shortening |
| 2 | cups buttermilk |

Dissolve the yeast in warm water. Set aside.

Combine the flour, sugar, baking powder, soda and salt in a large bowl. Cut in the shortening with a pastry blender. Make a well in the center of the flour mixture.

Add the buttermilk to the yeast mixture. Mix well with a wooden spoon. Turn onto floured board and knead gently, about 10 minutes.

Roll dough to ½ inch thickness and cut with a biscuit cutter. Place biscuits on an ungreased cookie sheet. Bake in a preheated 400 degree oven for 15 minutes.

# Strawberry Bread

| | |
|---|---|
| 1½ | cups flour |
| ½ | teaspoon baking soda |
| ½ | teaspoon salt |
| 1 | teaspoon cinnamon |
| 1 | cup sugar |
| 2 | eggs |
| 1 | (10 ounce) package frozen sliced strawberries (do not drain) |
| ⅝ | cups cooking oil |
| ⅝ | cups chopped pecans (optional) |

Mix flour, soda, salt, cinnamon, and sugar. Set aside.

Mix eggs, strawberries, oil and pecans. Add to dry ingredients. Stir carefully.

Turn batter into a greased loaf pan. Bake at 350 degrees for 1 hour and 15 minutes. Cool in pans for 10 minutes. Turn out onto a cooling rack.

# Dill Bread

*This recipe requires a bread machine*

1¼ cups buttermilk
2 tablespoons butter or margarine
2 tablespoons sugar
1½ teaspoons dill weed
1 teaspoon salt
⅛ teaspoon white pepper
3 cups white bread flour
2-3 teaspoons dry yeast

Add the ingredients in order or follow your bread machine directions.

# Dilly Bread

1 package dry yeast
¼ cup warm water
1 cup cottage cheese
2 tablespoons sugar
1 tablespoon instant onions
1 tablespoon dill seed
1 teaspoon salt
1 unbeaten egg
2¼ cups flour

Soften yeast in warm water. Heat cottage cheese to lukewarm. In large bowl combine cottage cheese, sugar, instant onion, dill seed, salt and egg. Mix well. Add softened yeast. Gradually add flour, beating well.

Place in greased bowl. Cover and let rise about an hour or until doubled. Stir down and put in greased, 1½ quart ovenproof casserole dish. Let rise 30-40 minutes. Bake at 350 degrees 40-50 minutes. Serves 10-12

# One Minute Bread

3 cups self-rising flour
⅓ cup sugar
1 (12 ounce) can of beer

Mix flour with sugar and add beer. Stir only until dry ingredients are moistened. Dough may not look smooth. Pour into a regular size greased bread pan. Bake at 350 degrees for 1 hour.

*This recipe is quick to make and does not require rising time. Bread can be frozen after it is baked.*

# Irish Soda Bread

3 cups flour
½ cup sugar
3 teaspoons baking powder
1 level teaspoon baking soda
½ teaspoon salt
1 cup currants or raisins
1 egg
2 teaspoons melted shortening
1¾ buttermilk

Combine flour, sugar, baking powder, soda, salt and raisins. Set aside.

In another bowl combine egg, shortening and buttermilk. Mix well and then add to the flour mixture. Mix well.

Turn into a greased 5x9-inch loaf pan and bake in a preheated 350 degree oven for 1 hour.

# Hearty Oatmeal Bread
*This recipe requires a bread machine*

½ cup apple juice
¾ cup water
2 tablespoons brown sugar
1 tablespoon shortening or diet margarine
1 teaspoon salt
2⅔ cups white bread flour
½ cup quick cooking oats
2-3 teaspoons dry yeast

Add the ingredients in order or follow your bread machine directions.

# Date Nut Bread

1 cup chopped dates
1 teaspoon baking soda
1 cup hot water
1 cup sugar
2 cups flour
1 egg
½ cup chopped walnuts
1 teaspoon vanilla
½ teaspoon salt
1 tablespoon melted shortening

Grease a 9x5-inch loaf pan.

Cut up dates. Sprinkle with baking soda and cover with hot water. Let stand 10 minutes.

Add sugar, flour egg, salt, vanilla, melted shortening and walnuts. Stir by hand until well mixed. Put in loaf pan. Bake at 350 degrees for 1 hour. Remove from pan immediately.

83

# Luscious Lemon Bread

| | |
|---|---|
| 2 | sticks butter |
| 2 | cups sugar |
| 4 | eggs |
| ½ | teaspoon salt |
| ½ | teaspoon baking soda |
| 3 | cups flour, sifted |
| 1 | cup buttermilk |
| | grated rind (zest) of one lemon |
| 1 | cup pecans, chopped |
| 2 | lemons, juice only |
| 1 | cup powdered sugar |

Cream butter and sugar. Blend in eggs.

Sift together soda, salt, and flour. Add alternately with buttermilk. Add lemon zest and nuts. Pour batter into two greased 7x3-inch loaf pans.

Bake at 300 degrees for 45 minutes. Bread is done when straw or toothpick inserted in center comes out clean.

Glaze: Mix lemon juice and powdered sugar well. Punch holes in bread with toothpick and pour glaze over while still warm from the oven.

# Pumpkin Fruit Bread

| | |
|---|---|
| 2 | cups sugar |
| 1 | cup vegetable oil |
| 3 | eggs |
| 1 | (16 ounce) can cooked pumpkin |
| 3 | cups all-purpose flour |
| 1 | teaspoon baking soda |
| ½ | teaspoon salt |
| ½ | teaspoon baking powder |
| 1 | teaspoon cinnamon |
| 1 | teaspoon ground cloves |
| 1 | teaspoon ground nutmeg |
| 1 | cup chopped nuts |
| 1 | cup raisins |
| 1 | cup chopped dates |

In a large mixing bowl beat together sugar and oil. Add eggs and continue beating until light and fluffy. Add pumpkin and mix well. Sift together flour, soda, salt, baking powder, cinnamon, cloves and nutmeg and add to pumpkin mixture. Stir until dry ingredients are moistened.

Fold in nuts, raisins and dates and pour into two 9x5-inch loaf pans greased with vegetable cooking spray. Bake at 325 degrees for 60-70 minutes or until a wooden pick inserted in center comes out clean. Leave loaves in pans for 10 minutes before removing. Cool on wire racks.

# Squash Bread

1½ cups flour, unsifted
2 teaspoons cinnamon
1 teaspoon baking powder
2 eggs
¾ cup sugar
½ cup oil
2 teaspoons vanilla
1⅓ cups coarsely shredded, lightly packed zucchini or yellow summer squash

Preheat oven to 325 degrees. Grease a 9x5-inch loaf pan. Mix flour, cinnamon and baking powder. In mixer bowl beat eggs until frothy. Add sugar, oil and vanilla. Beat until lemon colored, about 3 minutes. Stir in squash. Add dry ingredients. Mix until moistened. Pour into loaf pan. Bake for 55 minutes or until toothpick inserted in center of loaf comes out clean. Cool on rack for 10 minutes before removing from pan.

# Applesauce Spice Muffins

1 cup butter or margarine melted
2 cups sugar
2 eggs
2 cups applesauce
4 cups all-purpose flour
2 teaspoons baking soda
1 teaspoon salt
1 tablespoon ground cinnamon
2 teaspoons ground allspice
½ teaspoon ground cloves
1 cup chopped nuts
¼ cup powdered sugar

Cream butter, gradually add the 2 cups of sugar beating well at medium speed with an electric mixer. Add eggs, one at a time, beating well after each addition. Add applesauce, mixing well.

Combine flour, baking soda, salt, cinnamon, allspice, and cloves. Stir into batter. Stir in pecans. Fill greased miniature (1¾ inch) muffin pans about three-fourths full.

Bake at 350 degrees for 14 minutes until done. Transfer from pans to wire racks; sprinkle with powdered sugar. Makes 7 dozen

*Batter will keep in refrigerator for two weeks.*

# French Bread

1 cup lukewarm water
1½ teaspoons salt
1 package yeast
1 tablespoon soft shortening
3½-3¾ cups sifted flour
sesame or poppy seeds

Combine water and salt; add yeast and stir until well dissolved. Add shortening. Stir in flour, one half cup at a time. Continue adding enough flour to make a stiff dough. When dough begins to leave the sides of the bowl, turn it out onto a lightly floured board. Knead until dough is smooth and elastic and does not stick to the board.

Place in a greased bowl, turning once. Cover with a damp cloth and let rise in a warm place until double in bulk (about 1½ to 2 hours).

Punch down, fold over edges, and turn upside down. Cover and let rise again until almost double (30-45 minutes).

Roll the dough into an oblong shape (about 15x10 inches). Starting from a wide side, roll the dough up tightly as you would for a jelly roll. Punch the edges together to seal. With a hand on each end of the roll, roll gently back and forth to lengthen the loaf and taper the ends.

Place loaf diagonally on a baking sheet that has been lightly greased and sprinkled with cornmeal. Make ¼ inch deep slashes at 2 inch intervals on top of loaf. Brush top with cold water and let stand, uncovered 1½ hours.

Brush again with cold water and bake in a preheated 425 degree oven for 10 minutes. Brush again with cold water, reduce oven temperature to 375 degrees and bake 10 minutes longer.

*(continued on next page)*

86

Brush with water a third time and sprinkle with sesame or poppy seeds. Continue baking 10-15 minutes longer or until golden brown.

*This may seem like a lot of trouble for a product you can buy easily, but it is worth the trouble if you want a French bread that is crusty on the outside, soft in the middle and tastes far better. For more glaze and less crustiness, in place of water, brush with one egg white, slightly beaten with one tablespoon water.*

## Parmesan Bread Sticks

| | |
|---|---|
| 1 | (11 ounce) package refrigerated soft breadsticks |
| 3 | tablespoons margarine |
| ¾ | cup grated parmesan cheese |

Separate the can of refrigerated breadsticks. Cut in half to make 16 breadsticks.

Dip into melted margarine. Coat with parmesan.

Place on an ungreased cookie sheet. Bake at 350 degrees for 14-18 minutes or until golden brown.

*May be twisted and shaped into candy canes.*

## Anise Toast

| | |
|---|---|
| 1 | cup sugar |
| 3 | eggs |
| 1 | egg yolk |
| ¼ | cup butter |
| 2½ | cups sifted flour |
| 1½ | teaspoons anise extract |
| ¼ | minced aniseed |
| 2 | teaspoons baking powder |

Cream eggs, sugar and butter. Sift in flour, blend well. Add anise extract, aniseed and baking powder. Bake in buttered jelly roll pan at 350 degrees for 20 minutes. Cool. Cut in triangles. Brush with egg yolk. Bake on a cookie sheet for 2-3 minutes until lightly toasted.

# Doughnut Muffins

⅓ cup soft shortening
1 cup sugar, divided
1 egg
1½ cups sifted all- purpose
    flour
1½ teaspoon baking powder
½ teaspoon orange extract
½ teaspoon salt
½ cup milk, whole or
    2 percent
6 tablespoons melted butter
1 teaspoon cinnamon

Cream shortening and ½ cup sugar, add egg, beating well. Add the orange extract.

Combine flour and salt. Add alternately with milk to egg mixture.

Fill greased muffin pans two thirds full.

Bake at 350 degrees until golden brown (20-30 minutes). Remove from pan while hot and roll in melted butter and then in a mixture of ½ cup sugar and cinnamon. Makes 12 medium muffins

# Popovers

2 eggs
1 cup flour
1 cup milk
½ teaspoon salt

Heat oven to 450 degrees.

Generously grease six 6-ounce custard cups or 8 medium muffin cups.

Beat eggs slightly, beat in flour, milk, and salt just until smooth (do not over beat.)

Fill custard cups about ½ full, muffin cups about ¾ full. Bake 20 minutes.

Decrease oven temperature to 350 degrees.

Bake custard cups 20 minutes longer, muffin cups 15 minutes longer.

Immediately remove from cups. Serve hot.

Soups
and
Salads

# Tortilla Soup

| | |
|---|---|
| 1 | small onion, chopped |
| 1 | small green pepper, chopped |
| 1 | fresh jalapeño pepper, minced |
| 2 | cloves garlic, minced |
| 2 | tablespoons vegetable oil |
| 1 | large tomato, peeled and chopped |
| 1 | (12 ounce) can beef broth |
| 1 | (12 ounce) can chicken broth |
| 1½ | cups water |
| 1½ | cups tomato juice |
| 1 | tablespoon steak sauce |
| 1 | teaspoon salt |
| 2 | teaspoons Worcestershire sauce |
| ⅛ | teaspoon black pepper |
| 1 | teaspoon chili powder |
| 1 | teaspoon cumin |
| 3 | corn tortillas |
| | grated cheese, optional |

Sauté first four ingredients in the vegetable oil until soft. Add the rest of the ingredients, except the grated cheese and tortillas. Bring to a boil and simmer covered for one hour. Cut tortillas into strips. Add to soup and simmer for 10 minutes. Serve topped with grated cheddar cheese if desired.

# Sausage Bean Soup

| | |
|---|---|
| ½ | pound sausage |
| 1 | (16 ounce) can Italian tomatoes, cut up |
| 1 | (16 ounce) can Great Northern beans |
| 2 | cups water |
| 1 | small onion, diced |
| 1 | bay leaf |
| ¼ | teaspoon dried thyme |
| ¼ | teaspoon garlic salt |
| ½ | cup diced potatoes |
| ¼ | cup diced green pepper |

In skillet, sauté sausage until lightly browned, breaking up into small bite-size pieces. Drain off fat. Place in saucepan. Add cut up tomatoes and juice, Great Northern beans with liquid, water, onions, bay leaf, thyme and garlic salt.

Cover and simmer one hour. Add potatoes and green pepper. Cook until potatoes are tender. Serves 6-8

90

*Photo on right ~*
Black Bean and Corn Salad,
page 108

# Chicken-White Bean Soup

vegetable cooking spray
1    tablespoon olive oil
2    (4 ounce) skinned, boned chicken breasts, chopped
1    (3 ounce) piece Canadian bacon, chopped
¼    cup chopped onion
3    cloves garlic, minced
1    (13½ ounce) can chicken broth
1    (4 ounce) can chopped green chilies, undrained
¾    cup water
½    teaspoon ground coriander
¼    teaspoon ground cumin
⅛    teaspoon ground white pepper
2    (16 ounce) cans beans: white navy or great northern beans or 1 of each, drained
¼    cup shredded Monterey Jack cheese for garnish

Coat a large saucepan or Dutch oven with cooking spray. Add oil. Cook chicken and next 3 ingredients 3 minutes or until chicken is done.

Remove chicken mixture from pan and set aside. Add broth, chilies, water, coriander, cumin, and ground pepper to pan. Bring to a boil, reduce heat, and simmer 10 minutes. Add chicken mixture and beans and cook 5 minutes or until thoroughly heated.

Serve in individual bowls garnished with 2 teaspoons cheese. Serves 6

*Great Southwest-tasting soup that can be made ahead and frozen.*

*Photo on left ~*
Don't Sit on the Grass
Fire Ant Territory, page 10

# Cantrell Chili

2 pounds ground beef (preferably 1 pound ground beef and 1 pound smoked, chopped brisket)
1 medium onion, chopped
1 (8 ounce) can tomato sauce
2 (8 ounce) cans water
1 tablespoon salt
½ cup chili powder
¼ cup ground cumin
1 cup cooked pinto beans, optional
1 (8 ounce) jar chunky Mexican salsa, optional
shredded cheddar cheese for garnish, optional

In a heavy saucepan or Dutch oven, sear the ground beef over high heat until the meat becomes gray.

Drain excess grease from pan. If using 1 pound of chopped brisket, add after the grease has been drained. Add onion, tomato sauce, water, salt, chili powder, and cumin.

Cover the pan and simmer for about 1½ hours, stirring occasionally. During this time taste the chili, adding more cumin or salt, depending on your taste. The meat should become very tender as it cooks.

After the meat is tender, you may add the beans and/or salsa. Simmer about 30 minutes. Chili is best if it chills overnight, allowing all the flavors to mix together. Reheat the next day and serve piping hot with shredded cheese on top. Serves 6-8

*You may substitute ground turkey, chicken or venison to make up the 2 pounds of meat. If you are entertaining a large group, set up a serving line with corn chips, cooked rice, shredded lettuce, chili, salsa, jalapeño peppers, and shredded cheese. Allow guests to layer ingredients in their individual bowls. Winner of one First Place and two Second Place Awards at the Grapevine, Texas, Chamber of Commerce Chili Cook-Off*

# Shrimp and Corn Chowder

| | |
|---|---|
| ½ | pound shrimp |
| 1 | medium onion, chopped |
| 1 | stalk celery |
| 1 | (14 ounce) can creamed corn |
| ¼-½ | red bell pepper, chopped |
| 2 | bay leaves |
| 1 | small potato, cubed |
| | seafood seasoning |
| 1 | tablespoon parsley, minced |
| 1 | can chicken broth, if needed for additional liquid |

Peel and devein shrimp and set aside. Boil shrimp peels and seasonings with enough water to cover; strain stock. Sauté vegetables in butter. Add stock, corn, bay leaves and cubed potato. Simmer 30 minutes, and then add raw shrimp that have been cut in pieces. Cook until shrimp turn pink. Add parsley. Add a little milk and flour to thicken. Add chicken broth if needed. Serves 2-3

# South Carolina Frogmore Stew

| | |
|---|---|
| 1 | 4 inch smoked sausage link, sliced |
| ¾ | pound raw, unpeeled shrimp |
| 1 | ear corn |
| ¼ | small onion |
| 1 | small new potato |
| | crab boil seasoning, per directions |
| ½ | (12 ounce) can beer |

Fill pot with enough water to cover ingredients (2 parts water to one part beer). Add crab boil, potato, onion and sausage. Bring to a boil. Cover and reduce heat. Simmer 20 minutes. Add corn and cook about 10 more minutes. Add shrimp and cook about 3 minutes more. Drain. Adjust cooking time for large quantities. Shrimp are done when opaque. Makes one serving. Increase ingredients according to number of servings needed.

*Name comes from a small coastal town in South Carolina, Frogmore, where this dish is popular. Good for casual, outdoor summer supper. Cover picnic table with newspaper and let guests peel their own shrimp.*

# Burgoo

*A frontier dish or hunter's stew made from what was available*

1 (4½-5 pound) stewing chicken, quartered

4 cups beef broth or 2 (13¾ ounce) cans beef broth plus enough water to make 4 cups

2½ pounds ripe plum tomatoes, cut up or one (35 ounce) can of tomatoes

2 medium size onions, unpeeled and root end trimmed

1 tablespoon pepper

2 teaspoons curry powder

1 teaspoon salt

1½ cups bourbon

¾ pound skinless, boned chicken breasts, cut into 1-inch cubes

1 cup diced country ham trimmings or other smoked ham

2 cups fresh corn kernels or 1 (10 ounce) package frozen corn kernels

2 cups fresh lima beans or 1 (10 ounce) package frozen baby limas

1 cup diced, peeled raw potato

1 pound fresh okra, trimmed and halved lengthwise or 1 (10 ounce) package frozen okra

1 tablespoon filé powder, optional

Place chicken and beef broth in large saucepot; add enough water to cover chicken. Bring to boil over high heat. Reduce heat; cover and simmer until broth is clear, skimming off foam as necessary, about 20-30 minutes. When no more foam collects on top of broth, add tomato, onion, pepper, curry powder and salt. Cover partially and simmer gently for 2 hours. Add 1 cup of the bourbon. Simmer, partially covered, 2 hours longer.

Turn off heat. Remove chicken. Strain stock through food mill or sieve into another container, pressing onion and tomato pulp into broth. Discard solids. Chill until fat can be easily skimmed from surface. You should have about 8 cups of broth. If volume is greater, reduce to 8 cups. When chicken is cool enough to handle, remove and discard skin and bones. Reserve meat in large pieces. The burgoo can be made ahead up to this point and refrigerated for 24 hours.

Rinse saucepot. Pour in strained broth; add remaining ½ cup bourbon. Bring to boiling. Add raw chicken breast, ham, corn, lima beans, potato and okra; bring to boiling. Lower heat; partially cover and simmer 30 minutes. Add cooked chicken pieces; heat to serving temperature. Remove

*(continued on next page)*

pot from heat. If burgoo is not as thick as you wish, stir in filé powder. Serves 16

*If a roaster chicken is used instead of a stewing chicken, remove from broth after 2 hours. If filé powder is used, add it only after the pot is off the heat and only to the amount you plan to serve. Reheated burgoo containing filé will be gummy and stringy.*

# Scallop Soup

| | |
|---|---|
| 2 | (8 ounce) bottles clam juice |
| 1 | tablespoon unsalted butter |
| ½ | teaspoon Worcestershire sauce |
| ½ | teaspoon dry mustard |
| 1 | tablespoon finely minced celery leaves |
| | salt and white pepper |
| ¾-1 | pound bay scallops (tiny) |
| 2 | egg yolks |
| 1 | cup heavy cream |
| ¼ | cup dry white wine |
| 2 | tablespoons minced fresh parsley |

Put clam juice and butter in a sauce-pan and let simmer. Add Worcestershire, mustard, celery leaves, a little salt if needed, and some freshly ground white pepper. When mixture is about to boil, add scallops and simmer 3-4 minutes.

Beat egg yolks with cream and then stir a little hot broth into them. Stir egg/cream mixture into soup and continue to simmer 2 minutes more. Add wine, bring just to boiling point, and serve with parsley sprinkled into each bowl. Serves 6-8

*White vermouth for white wine is delicious. This soup does not freeze well and must be served immediately. Small servings make a great begin-ning to an elegant dinner party. Large servings are great for Sunday night supper, along with crusty bread and a green salad.*

# Artichoke Cheddar Soup

| | |
|---|---|
| 1 | cup chopped onions |
| 1 | cup chopped carrots |
| 1 | cup chopped celery |
| ½ | cup butter |
| ½ | cup flour |
| 2 | tablespoons cornstarch |
| 4 | cups chicken broth |
| 4 | cups milk |
| 2 | cups shredded Cheddar cheese |
| 1 | teaspoon freshly ground pepper |
| 2 | (14 ounce) cans artichoke hearts, drained, cut into fourths |
| | salt to taste |

Sauté onions, carrots and celery in the butter in a stockpot until tender. Stir in flour and cornstarch. Add chicken broth and milk. Cook over medium heat until the mixture begins to boil and thicken, stirring frequently; reduce heat. Add cheese and pepper. Simmer until the cheese is melted, stirring frequently. Stir in artichoke hearts and salt. Ladle the warm soup into soup bowls. Serves 6-8

# Tomato Basil Soup

| | |
|---|---|
| 4 | cups tomatoes, peeled, cored and chopped (about 8-10 tomatoes) |
| 3 | cups tomato juice |
| 1 | cup chicken broth |
| 12-14 | washed fresh basil leaves |
| 1 | cup half-and-half |
| ¼ | pound sweet unsalted butter |
| | white pepper to taste |
| | lemon zest |

Combine tomatoes, tomato juice and chicken broth in a 4 quart saucepan. Simmer, covered for 30 minutes. Puree, along with the basil leaves, in small batches, in blender or food processor.

Return to saucepan and add butter, Half-and-half, white pepper and lemon zest while stirring over low heat. This can be prepared ahead. Garnish with a large crouton and additional basil and lemon zest. Serves 6-8

*Cream may be used instead of half-and half. Canned whole tomatoes, crushed, may be used instead of fresh tomatoes. Two chicken bouillon cubes may be used instead of chicken broth.*

96

# Chicken Chili and Lime Soup

6 cups rich chicken stock
10 mild green chilies, seeded and diced or 1 large can chopped green chilies
3 large ripe tomatoes, peeled and diced
1 small onion, diced
2 green onion, thinly sliced
2 large jalapeños, seeded and diced
1 pound canned tomatillos, diced or 1 pound fresh, peeled and diced
2 chicken breasts, cooked and shredded
8 artichoke hearts, chopped
2 small limes, juiced
1 tablespoon ground cumin
1 tablespoon fresh chopped parsley
  salt and pepper to taste
  seasoned croutons
¾ cup Muenster cheese, grated

Place all ingredients, except cheese, in a large soup pot. Cook over medium heat for 30 minutes. Spoon soup into individual ovenproof bowls. Top with croutons, grated cheese and broil until cheese is bubbly. Serve immediately. Serves 6

*Can be prepared 1-3 days ahead, but does not freeze well.*

# Gazpacho Blanco

1 cucumber, peeled, seeded and cut into chunks
½ cup chicken broth
½ cup sour cream, or plain yogurt
1 clove garlic
2-3 teaspoons white wine vinegar, or to taste
  salt
  tomato, chopped
  green onion, chopped

Combine all ingredients except tomato and green onion in processor or blender and mix until smooth. Pour into serving bowls. Sprinkle with chopped tomato and chopped green onion before serving. Serves 1-2

# Garlic Soup

| | |
|---|---|
| 1 | medium onion, thinly sliced |
| 5 | cloves garlic, or to taste |
| 2 | tablespoons olive oil |
| 2 | medium potatoes, diced |
| 4 | cups beef stock |
| 1 | (8 ounce) can tomato sauce or coarsely chopped tomatoes |
| ½ | teaspoon dried basil |
| ½ | teaspoon dried thyme |
| ½ | teaspoon dried parsley |

In 3-quart saucepan, sauté onion and garlic oil over low heat. When onion is golden, add potatoes. Cook 3 minutes over medium heat. Add beef stock, tomato sauce (or tomatoes) and herbs. Stir well. Cook until potatoes are done but still firm (10-15 minutes). Garnish with fresh parsley, Parmesan cheese and croutons if desired. Serves 4-6

*Great when made 2 days ahead for flavors to mingle. It freezes well.*

# Southwest Chicken Soup

| | |
|---|---|
| 1 | cup chopped onion |
| ½ | cup chopped celery |
| 1 | tablespoon olive oil |
| 6 | cups chicken stock |
| 4 | chicken breast halves |
| 4 | chicken thighs |
| ½ | cup brown rice |
| 1 | (10 ounce) package frozen cut corn |
| 1 | teaspoon cumin |
| 1 | tablespoon chili powder |
| 2 | tablespoons picante sauce |
| 1 | (15½ ounce) can diced tomatoes |
| 1 | (4 ounce) can chopped green chilies |

In a soup kettle, sauté onions and celery in oil until soft. Add chicken stock, chicken pieces and brown rice. Bring mixture to a boil. Reduce heat, cover and simmer until chicken is tender, 20-30 minutes. Remove chicken and set aside to cool. Continue simmering for an additional 15 minutes. Remove chicken from the bones and add to the stock along with remaining ingredients. Heat through; adjust seasoning to taste. Serves 6-8

# Belgian Asparagus Soup

2 bunches asparagus
1 large onion, chopped
4 stalks celery, chopped
2 tablespoons butter
2 tablespoons chopped garlic
¼ ounce fresh thyme or 1 tablespoon dried
½ ounce fresh parsley or 2 tablespoons dried
½ bunch fresh spinach, shopped
4 ounces heavy cream (optional)
1 quart chicken stock
salt to taste
pepper to taste

Remove tough ends from asparagus, reserve several tips for garnish, and chop the rest of the asparagus into small slices and set aside. Place chopped onion and celery in a large pot with butter and sauté over low heat until onions are soft and translucent (about 10 minutes). Add garlic, thyme, parsley, salt, and pepper. Cover with chicken broth and bring to a boil. Add asparagus to boiling broth and cook until asparagus is tender (about 7 minutes). Strain hot mixture, saving broth. Puree vegetables in food processor, adding spinach for color. Return pureed vegetables to broth, add seasonings and cream, and heat to serving temperature (do not boil after cream has been added). Serve in a tureen or in individual bowls with reserved asparagus tips for garnish.

# Cold Cream of Raspberry Soup

1½ quarts fresh or frozen raspberries
1 cup heavy cream
1 cup milk
½ cup water
2 sprigs Irish mint
¾ ounce orange base liqueur
juice of ½ lemon
1 cup powdered sugar
lime to garnish
sour cream to garnish

Place all ingredients in food processor and blend for 1 minute. Pour into stainless steel bowl and refrigerate for 1 hour. Pour soup into chilled soup cups and float a lime slice on top of soup with a dab of sour cream and raspberry to garnish. Serves 5

## Pumpkin Soup

| | |
|---|---|
| 1 | tablespoon olive oil |
| 4 | sweet Italian sausage (from deli counter) |
| 1 | small onion, chopped |
| 2 | stalks celery, chopped |
| ½ | pound sliced mushrooms or 1 (8 ounce) can |
| 2 | cloves fresh garlic, chopped |
| ½ | teaspoon sage |
| ½ | teaspoon rosemary salt and pepper to taste |
| 1 | cup Marsala wine |
| 1 | can pumpkin puree |
| 2 | cans chicken stock |

Slice sausages (½ inch thick). Brown with onion in olive oil. Add celery. Cook until soft. Add mushrooms (if fresh, cook until soft), spices, wine, pumpkin and stock. Simmer 30 minutes until thickened. Spices may be adjusted to taste. Serves 6

## Spicy Baked Potato Soup

| | |
|---|---|
| 6-8 | slices bacon, fried crisp, drippings reserved |
| 1 | cup diced yellow onions |
| ⅔ | cup flour |
| 6 | cups hot chicken stock |
| 4 | cups diced, peeled baked potatoes |
| 2 | cups half-and-half |
| ⅛ | cup dried, chopped parsley |
| 1½ | teaspoon garlic powder |
| 1½ | teaspoon dried basil |
| 1½ | teaspoon salt |
| 1½ | teaspoon pepper |
| 1 | teaspoon hot pepper sauce |
| 1 | cup grated cheddar |
| ½ | cup diced green onions |

Crumble bacon and set aside. Put remaining drippings in medium Dutch oven. Cook onions in drippings until transparent, 3 minutes. Add flour, stirring to prevent lumps. Cool 3-5 minutes until just golden. Add chicken broth gradually, whisking constantly to prevent lumps until thickened. Reduce to simmer. Add bacon and all ingredients except cheese and green onions. Simmer 10 minutes. Don't boil. Add cheese and onions until melted smoothly. Garnish with additional bacon and cheese. Must be served immediately and does not freeze well. Serves 6-8

100

# Mozzarella, Tomato and Fresh Basil Pesto

| | | |
|---|---|---|
| 4 | large beefsteak tomatoes | |
| 8 | ounces mozzarella cheese | |
| ½ | cup fresh basil pesto | |
| ¼-½ | cup virgin olive oil | |
| | salt | |
| | freshly ground pepper | |
| | lettuce | |

Cut each tomato into 4-6 slices. Cut Mozzarella cheese into the same number of slices of tomatoes. Pesto should be at room temperature. Divide tomato and cheese into 8 equal portions. Arrange 1 slice of cheese over each tomato slice. Spread thin layer of pesto over cheese. Continue layering in same order for each portion, ending with pesto. Arrange salad in circle on platter overlapping portions slightly. Serve at room temperature. Pass olive oil, salt and pepper separately. Serves 6-8

# Fresh Basil Pesto

| | |
|---|---|
| 2 | cups packed fresh basil leaves |
| 2 | large garlic cloves |
| ½ | cup pine nuts |
| ¾ | cup grated Romano cheese |
| ⅔ | cup olive oil |

Combine basil and garlic in processor work bowl and blend to fine paste, scraping down sides of bowl as necessary. Add pine nuts and cheese and process until smooth. With machine running, pour olive oil through feed tube in slow, steady stream and mix until smooth and creamy. If pesto is too thick, gradually pour up to ¼ cup warm water through feed tube with machine running.

Transfer pesto to jar. Cover surface of pesto with film of olive oil about ⅛ inch thick. Seal jar with tight fitting lid.

Refrigerate up to 3 months or freeze. Stir oil into pesto before using.

# Company Salad with Raspberry Vinaigrette

| 1 | head Bibb lettuce, torn into bite-size pieces | Combine first six ingredients; toss with Raspberry vinaigrette. Serves 8 |

1 head Bibb lettuce, torn into bite-size pieces
½ pound fresh spinach
2 oranges, peeled and sectioned
2 Red Delicious apples, unpeeled and thinly sliced
1 kiwi fruit, thinly sliced
½ coarsely chopped walnuts
  raspberry vinaigrette

Combine first six ingredients; toss with Raspberry vinaigrette. Serves 8

## Raspberry Vinaigrette

½ cup vegetable oil
¼ cup raspberry vinegar
1 tablespoon honey
½ teaspoon grated orange rind
¼ teaspoon salt
⅛ teaspoon pepper

Combine in jar; cover tightly, shake vigorously. Chill thoroughly.

*Great at Christmas with red and green.*

# Spaghetti Salad

1 pound spaghetti, broken
1 green pepper, chopped
1 tomato, chopped
1 onion, chopped
1 cucumber, chopped
4 tablespoons Salad Supreme seasoning
1 (8 ounce) bottle of Italian dressing

Cook spaghetti, drain and cool. Add chopped vegetables and Salad Supreme. Toss. Add dressing and mix well. Let marinate in refrigerator overnight. Serves 8-10

# Pretzel Jello

| | |
|---|---|
| 2 | cups broken pretzels |
| 1½ | sticks margarine, melted |
| 1 | tablespoon sugar |
| 1 | (8 ounce) package cream cheese |
| 1 | (10 ounce) package frozen dairy topping |
| 1 | cup powdered sugar |
| 2 | cups boiling water |
| 1 | large package strawberry jello |
| 2 | (10 ounce) packages frozen strawberries |

Mix first 3 ingredients and press into a 9x13 pan. Bake at 350 degrees for 8 minutes.

Mix cream cheese, whipped topping and sugar and beat until creamy. Pour over cool crust and refrigerate until firm.

Dissolve jello in boiling water and add frozen strawberries. Let set 5-10 minutes to thicken and pour on top of cream cheese mixture. Serves 8

# Summer Fruit Salad

| | |
|---|---|
| 1 | fresh pineapple, peeled, cored and cubed |
| 1 | quart fresh, hulled strawberries |
| ½ | cup fresh or frozen raspberries, thawed |
| 1 | (11 ounce) can mandarin oranges, drained |
| ½ | cup fresh or frozen blueberries |
| 2 | cups orange juice |
| ½ | cup sugar |
| ¼ | cup cream sherry |
| ½ | teaspoon almond extract |
| ½ | teaspoon vanilla extract |

Combine first 5 ingredients in a large bowl. Combine remaining ingredients, stirring until sugar dissolves. Pour sherry mixture over fruit mixture, tossing lightly. Cover and chill 2-3 hours.

Serve with slotted spoon. Serves 8

# Secora's Salad

| 10-12 | oranges |
| 1 | cup raisins |
| ¼-½ | cup honey |
| ½-1 | teaspoon cinnamon (sprinkled lightly to taste) |

Slice oranges in ¼-inch slices. Remove orange peels. Place a layer of orange slices in bottom of 9x13 glass dish. Sprinkle approximately ¼ cup of raisins over oranges. Drizzle honey and sprinkle cinnamon over oranges and raisins. Layer oranges, raisins, honey and cinnamon until all ingredients are gone. Refrigerate 6 hours overnight. Serve chilled. Serves 16

*A squeeze bottle of honey makes preparation easier. A member first tasted this while cruising on a yacht off the California coast; it was served by her host's maid, Secora.*

# First Prize Caesar Salad

| 8 | anchovy fillets |
| 2 | egg yolks (from eggs cooked in shell in boiling water 1 minute) |
| 2 | tablespoons red wine vinegar |
| 2 | cloves garlic, minced |
| | juice of 1 lemon |
| ½ | teaspoon Thai red chili oil |
| ¼ | teaspoon Worcestershire sauce |
| 1 | tablespoon grated Asiago cheese |
| 1 | tablespoon grated Parmesan cheese |
| ½ | teaspoon truffle oil (optional) |
| ½ | cup olive oil |
| ½ | cup vegetable oil |
| | Romaine lettuce |
| | garlic croutons |

Blend anchovy, egg yolks, vinegar, garlic, lemon juice, red chili oil, Worcestershire sauce, grated cheeses in food processor. Add oils slowly. Refrigerate at least one hour before serving. Mix with lettuce, croutons and additional cheese. Serves 6-8

# Fresh Broccoli-Mandarin Salad

1    egg plus 1 egg yolk, slightly beaten
½    cup granulated sugar
1½   teaspoons cornstarch
1    teaspoon dry mustard
½    cup tarragon wine vinegar
¼    cup water
½    cup mayonnaise
3    tablespoons butter or margarine, softened
4    cups fresh broccoli flowerets
2    cups sliced fresh mushrooms
1    (11 ounce) can mandarin oranges, drained
½    cup raisins
½    cup slivered almonds toasted
½    large red onion, sliced
6    slices bacon, cooked and crumbled

In the top of a double boiler, whisk together egg, egg yolk, sugar, cornstarch, and dry mustard. Combine vinegar and water. Slowly pour into egg mixture, whisking constantly. Place over simmering water and cook, stirring constantly, until mixture thickens. Remove from heat; stir in mayonnaise and butter. Chill. To serve, toss dressing with broccoli, mushrooms, oranges, raisins, almonds, onion, and bacon in a serving bowl. Serves 10-12

# Grilled Summer Salad

1    cup red, yellow or green pepper strips
1    cup zucchini slices, ½ inch thick
⅓    cup red onion rings
1    tablespoon chopped oregano or ½ teaspoon dried
2    tablespoons olive oil
1    cup tomato wedges
¾    cup crumbled feta cheese
     salt and pepper to taste
     juice of 2 lemons

Wrap peppers, zucchini, onions, oregano and olive oil in double thickness foil. Grill 8-10 minutes. Place in a salad bowl. Add tomato. Toss with lemon juice, salt and pepper and feta cheese. Serves 6

# Spinach Salad with Creamy Mustard Dressing

1  pound spinach, rinsed, stemmed and torn into pieces
½  pound bacon, fried crisp, drained and crumbled
¼  pound mushrooms sliced
1  cup sliced water chestnuts
½  cup black olives sliced

In large bowl, combine all ingredients and toss well with Creamy Mustard Dressing. Serves 8-10

Creamy Mustard Dressing

2  hard cooked eggs, mashed with fork while still warm
½  teaspoon salt
1½  teaspoon sugar
1  tablespoon coarsely ground black pepper
1  clove garlic, crushed
½  cup virgin olive oil
1  tablespoon Dijon mustard
5  tablespoons heavy cream
¼  cup red wine vinegar

One at a time and in order, thoroughly blend all other ingredients into mashed eggs. Do not substitute. When blended, whisk until smooth.

# Oriental Salad

1  pound of coleslaw mix
1  bunch green onions, chopped
¼  cup slivered almonds
¼  cup sunflower seeds
¼  cup raspberry vinegar
¼  cup salad oil
¼  cup sugar
3  teaspoons regular vinegar
1  (3 ounce) package beef flavored Ramen noodles, crushed

Mix first four ingredients together. Mix vinegars, oil and sugar together with beef flavored packet from noodle mix. Pour over other ingredients and toss. Refrigerate several hours. Top with dry noodles before serving. Serves 12

## Cole Slaw Surprise

| | |
|---|---|
| 2 | cups sugar |
| ½ | cup vinegar |
| 1 | teaspoon salt |
| ¼ | cup salad oil |
| ¼-¾ | teaspoon marjoram |
| 1 | (14-ounce) can sauerkraut (including juice) |
| 1 | cup chopped onions |
| 1 | cup chopped green pepper |
| 2 | cups chopped celery |
| 1 | jar chopped pimento or chopped red bell pepper |

Mix sugar, vinegar, salt, salad oil and marjoram, stirring well. Pour over vegetables and refrigerate overnight. Stir occasionally to blend flavors. Serves 8

## St. Simon Island Salade

| | |
|---|---|
| 2 | small heads Bibb lettuce, torn into bite-size pieces |
| 1 | head radicchio, torn into bite-size pieces |
| 1 | bunch watercress, stems removed |

Dressing

| | |
|---|---|
| 4 | tablespoons extra-virgin olive oil |
| 4 | tablespoons balsamic vinegar |
| | salt and pepper |
| 8-12 | slices (¼ inch thick) French bread, sliced |
| 8-12 | slices goat cheese (chèvre or provolone cheese, if desired) |

Combine greens in bowl. Chill. Mix dressing ingredients. Just before serving, melt cheese on top of toasted bread under broiler. Toss greens with dressing. Serve on individual salad plates topped with toasts. Serves 8

# Pear Walnut Salad

4 cups lettuce, torn into bite-sizes pieces
1 pear, cored, chopped or sliced
¼ cup toasted walnut halves
2 ounces bleu cheese, crumbled

Dressing
½ cup oil
3 tablespoons vinegar
¼ cup sugar
½ teaspoon celery seed
¼ teaspoon salt

In jar with tight-fitting lid, combine all dressing ingredients. Shake until well blended and sugar is dissolved. Refrigerate to blend flavors. To toast walnuts, spread on cookie sheet. Bake at 375 degrees for 3-5 minutes or until golden brown, stirring occasionally. Or, spread in thin layer in microwave-safe pan. Microwave on high for 3-4 minutes or until light golden brown, stirring frequently. In large bowl, combine all salad ingredients. Just before serving, pour dressing over salad; toss to coat. Serves 4

*For added color and fiber, leave skin on pears. Red apples also taste great in this salad.*

# Black Bean and Corn Salad served in Tomato Cups

1 (15 ounce) can sweet tender whole kernel corn, drained
1 (15 ounce) can black beans, rinsed and drained
½ cup green onions, chopped with bottoms
2 cloves garlic, minced
¼ cup cilantro, chopped
few shakes red pepper flakes
4 large firm ripe tomatoes
½ cup Italian dressing
fresh cracked pepper
salt

Drain canned vegetables and combine in bowl. Add onion, garlic, cilantro and red pepper. Toss well. Wash and cut tomatoes in half. Remove centers and chop well. Add chopped tomato to vegetable mixture and blend well. Pour dressing over vegetables and stir until coated well. More dressing may be added if needed Add fresh cracked pepper and salt. Cover salad and chill 3-4 hours. When ready to serve, spoon salad mixture into tomato halves. Serves 4

# Spinach Salad with Raspberry Cream Dressing

1 (10 ounce) package fresh
   spinach
2 kiwi fruit, peeled and
   sliced
1 (11 ounce) can mandarin
   oranges, drained
1 purple onion sliced and
   separated into rings
   Raspberry Cream Dressing

Remove stems from spinach; wash thoroughly, and pat dry. Tear into bite-size pieces. Combine spinach and next 3 ingredients in a large bowl; cover and chill. Serve with Raspberry Cream Dressing. Serves 6-8

Raspberry Cream Dressing
1 (10 ounce) package frozen
   raspberries, thawed and
   drained
6 tablespoons olive oil
¼ cup whipping cream
2 tablespoons sherry wine
   vinegar
½ teaspoon salt

Place raspberries in an electric blender; process until smooth. Pour through a wire-mesh strainer into a bowl; press mixture with back of a spoon against sides of strainer to squeeze out liquid. Discard seeds. Combine raspberry puree, olive oil, and remaining ingredients, whisking until smooth. Chill. Serve with salad. Makes 1½ cups

# Mom's Quick Potato Salad

5 new potatoes
½ cup mayonnaise-type
   salad dressing
1 teaspoon prepared
   mustard
   pickle juice or milk

Boil new potatoes in jackets and cool. Peel and slice. Mix next two ingredients and then with pickle juice or milk. Serves 2

# Summery Chicken Salad

6 cups chicken, cooked and chopped
1¼ cups sliced celery
1 (8 ounce) can pineapple tidbits, drained
1¼ cups reduced fat mayonnaise
¾ teaspoon salt
2½ tablespoons dry white wine
¾ teaspoon curry powder
1 cantaloupe, thinly sliced
1 pint strawberries
2 Red Delicious apples, thinly sliced
½ pound green grapes
1 cup blackberries
lettuce leaves
½ cup chopped walnuts, toasted

Combine chicken, celery and pineapple bits in large bowl; set aside. Combine mayonnaise, wine, salt, and curry powder. Add to chicken mixture, tossing to coat. Cover and refrigerate 1 to 2 hours. Arrange apples, cantaloupe, grapes, strawberries and blackberries on a lettuce lined platter; top with chicken mixture. Sprinkle with walnuts. Garnish, if desired. Serves 6

# Southwestern Grilled Chicken Salad

1 cup uncooked brown rice
1 cup uncooked white rice
1 cup cooked black beans
1 medium red pepper, chopped
1 medium green pepper, chopped
5 green onions, chopped
¼ cup fresh cilantro, chopped
⅓ cup peanut oil
¼ cup lime juice
salt and pepper
3 avocados
4 large boneless chicken breasts

Cook rice (brown and white separately) according to directions. Cool to room temperature. Combine with next 5 ingredients. Whisk oil, lime juice in small bowl. Add salt and pepper. Pour over rice and toss well. Grill chicken breasts and chop 2 of the breasts. Add to rice mixture. Slice remaining breasts into long strips and place on top of salad alternately with sliced avocados for presentation.

# Curried Chicken and Pasta Salad

| | |
|---|---|
| 4 | boneless, skinless chicken breasts halves, cooked |
| ¼ | cup uncooked pasta |
| 2 | cups seedless red grapes |
| ¼ | cup thinly sliced celery |
| ¼ | cup thinly sliced green onion |
| 2½ | tablespoons plain low-fat yogurt |
| ¾ | cup low-fat mayonnaise |
| 1½ | tablespoons honey |
| 1½ | teaspoons lemon juice |
| ¼ | teaspoon curry powder |
| ½ | teaspoon salt |
| | freshly ground black pepper to taste |
| | lettuce to garnish |

Cook pasta according to package directions; drain, set aside. Cut chicken into 1 inch chunks; place in a large bowl. Add grapes, celery, green onion and pasta, set aside. In a small bowl, blend yogurt, salad dressing, honey, lemon juice, curry powder, salt and pepper. Pour over chicken mixture and gently toss. To serve, line a platter or serving bowl with lettuce leaves and spoon chicken salad onto lettuce. Serves 8 (¾ cup each)

# German Potato Salad

| | |
|---|---|
| 5 | pounds potatoes, cooked and diced |
| ½ | pound bacon and drippings |
| 3 | tablespoons flour |
| 1½ | cups sugar |
| 1½ | cups vinegar |
| 1½ | cups water |
| 1 | onion, chopped |
| 2 | ribs celery, chopped |
| ½ | green pepper (optional) |

Fry bacon. Add flour and sugar to drippings and stir. Add vinegar and water and boil 8 minutes. Salt and pepper to taste. Add potatoes, bacon, onion, and celery. Stir well. Refrigerate. Warm to serve.

111

# Almond Chicken Salad

| | |
|---|---|
| 4 | whole chicken breasts |
| 1 | stalk celery |
| 2 | tablespoons butter |
| 1 | cup blanched almonds |
| 2 | red apples |
| ½ | pound bacon |
| 2 | tablespoons fresh lemon juice |
| 1 | cup mayonnaise |
| 2-3 | tablespoons curry powder |
| ½ | cup chopped celery |
| 2 | heads Bibb lettuce, separated |
| | watercress or parsley sprigs |

Place chicken breasts in large saucepan with approximately 2 quarts of water to cover. Add celery stalk and simmer for 25-30 minutes. Remove from liquid and set aside to cool. Discard liquid.

Melt the butter over medium heat, add almonds and sauté them until golden brown, stirring constantly about 3-4 minutes. Remove with slotted spoon and drain/cool on paper towels.

Wash, core and chop apples into small pieces and sprinkle with lemon juice to prevent discoloration.

Skin and bone chicken and cut into bite-sized pieces.

In a 10 inch skillet, cook bacon until crisp and set aside on paper towels to drain. Crumble bacon and set aside.

In a small bowl combine mayonnaise and curry until well blended.

In a large mixing bowl, combine chicken, almonds, apple, celery and dressing. Toss lightly to coat.

Serve as individual salads on beds of Bibb lettuce or a large chilled platter decorated with Bibb lettuce. Garnish with crumbled bacon and watercress or parsley sprigs. Serves 6-8

# Oriental Chicken Salad

4   cups torn greens, iceberg
    or romaine
3   ounces dry Chinese
    noodles
2   cooked chicken breasts,
    chopped
8   tablespoons sliced al-
    monds
8   tablespoons chopped
    green onions
8   tablespoons sesame seeds
    red pepper to taste
8   ounces dressing

Dressing
⅝   cup (10 tablespoons) rice
    vinegar
2½  tablespoons soy sauce
7   tablespoons granulated
    sugar
2   teaspoons ground mustard
    pepper to taste
7   tablespoons peanut oil
1½  tablespoons sesame soy
    oil
1½  tablespoons sesame seeds

Toss salad ingredients together. Mix dressing in shaker bottle and dress salad to taste. Refrigerate unused portion of dressing. Serves 4

# Ziti Salad with Sausage or Pepperoni

12 ounces ziti or other tubular pasta

2 pounds salami or pepperoni, thinly sliced

1 pound zucchini, thinly sliced

4 medium tomatoes, cut in wedges

1 medium green bell pepper, coarsely chopped

1 cup minced fresh parsley

3 ounces chopped pimento chopped red onion and calamata olives, optional

Dressing

⅓ cup red wine vinegar

½ teaspoon salt

¼ teaspoon fresh ground pepper

⅛ teaspoon cayenne pepper

¼ teaspoon rosemary, crumbled

¼ teaspoon oregano, crumbled

¼ teaspoon basil, crumbled

1⅓ olive oil

¼ cup freshly grated Parmesan cheese

Combine vinegar, seasonings and herbs in a small bowl. Whisk in oil in slow, steady stream until well blended. Mix in Parmesan cheese and set dressing aside. Cook pasta al dente (approximately 8 minutes) in 4-6 quarts boiling salted water. Drain and rinse under cold water until cool. Drain again . Combine pasta and remaining ingredients except Parmesan, in a large bowl. Add half the dressing and toss. Add as much of the remaining dressing as necessary to coat salad thoroughly. Sprinkle with additional Parmesan if desired, and serve. Serves 8-12

*Does not keep since zucchini becomes bitter.*

114

# Strawberry Chicken Salad

| | | |
|---|---|---|
| 1 | head Romaine lettuce torn in pieces | |
| 1 | bunch green onions sliced | |
| 1 | (8 ounce) package sliced mushrooms | |
| 1 | pint strawberries, sliced | |
| 1 | cup seedless green grapes | |
| 4 | chicken breasts, poached and chilled and cut into bite-sized pieces | |
| ½ | cup slivered almonds, lightly toasted | |

Dressing
| | |
|---|---|
| 1½ | cups sugar |
| 2 | teaspoons dry mustard |
| 2 | teaspoons salt |
| ⅔ | cup apple cider vinegar |
| ½ | medium onion (white or purple) |
| 2 | cups vegetable oil |
| 3 | tablespoons poppy seeds |

Put all salad ingredients in a large salad bowl. Toss gently with dressing.

Put all ingredients for the dressing in a blender except oil and poppy seeds. (Mix ½ sugar at a time and ¼ onion at a time). While on high, add oil in stream until thick and milky. Add poppy seeds. Store in refrigerator. The dressing recipe makes enough for two salads (or more).

*The dressing keeps well. It is a great dressing for any fruit salad. A purple onion will give the dressing a lovely pink shade.*

# Old Fashioned Fruit Dressing

| | |
|---|---|
| 2 | eggs |
| 2 | tablespoons sugar |
| 2 | tablespoons lemon juice |
| 2 | tablespoons pineapple juice |
| 2 | tablespoons softened butter |
| | dash of salt |
| 8 | ounces whipping cream (whipped) or light dairy topping |

Beat first 6 ingredients together with a beater. Cook in saucepan over low heat. Cool. Fold in whipped cream. Makes 2 cups

*This is great on fresh fruit salad. It is a Cajun recipe from New Orleans obtained 30 years ago and enjoyed by all who have tried it.*

115

# Tortellini Shrimp Salad

2   (8 ounce) packages tri-
    colored tortellini
    stuffed with Parmesan
    cheese
1   pound cooked shrimp,
    peeled
⅓   cup grated Romano
    cheese
4   green onions, finely sliced
⅓   cup chopped red bell
    pepper
1   tablespoon dried basil
Dressing
¼   cup red wine vinegar
2   tablespoons water
1   tablespoon canola oil
1   tablespoon dried basil
1   tablespoon Dijon mustard

Cook tortellini according to directions on package omitting salt and oil. Drain well and cool slightly. In a large bowl, combine remaining ingredients. Combine all dressing ingredients together. Add to salad and toss. Serve or keep in refrigerator. Best when served at room temperature. Serves 8

# Sweet and Sour Dressing for Spinach Salad

½   cup sugar (super fine-bar
    sugar)
½   teaspoon salt
1   teaspoon dry mustard
1   teaspoon grated onion
¼   cup tarragon vinegar
¾   cup vegetable oil
Spinach Salad
1   bag spinach leaves, torn
    into bite-sized pieces
1   pound bacon, fried crispy
    and crumbled
1   pound fresh mushrooms,
    sliced
6   hard boiled eggs, sliced
1   small red onion, sliced

Place dressing ingredients (except oil), in blender and blend for 3 minutes. Turn blender on lowest setting and add oil in a thin stream. Blend until creamy; about 2 minutes. Chill until ready to use. Will keep refrigerated for 2 weeks. Add to spinach salad when ready to serve. Serves 8

# Perfecto Pasta Salad

| | |
|---|---|
| 1 | pound imported pasta, preferably penne |
| 2 | jars marinated artichokes, drained and chopped |
| 1 | can hearts of palm, drained and chopped |
| 3 | small bell peppers (1 red, 1 yellow, 1 green) |
| ¾ | pound Mozzarella cheese, cut in ½ inch chunks or narrow strips |
| ½ | pound Monterey Jack jalapeño cheese, cut, in ½ inch chunks or narrow strips |
| 1 | (2.5 ounce) can sliced ripe olives |
| ½ | pound sliced Pepperoni cut in slices |
| ½ | (10 ounce) package frozen English peas |
| 4-5 | carrots, sliced in disks |
| ½-1 | cup dried Roma tomatoes, or fresh |
| ¼ | cup fresh basil, finely chopped |
| | extra virgin olive oil |
| | imported balsamic vinegar |
| | salt and pepper to taste |
| | dash garlic |

Cook penne al dente. (The literal translation of al dente is "to the teeth"). Drain the pasta well and place in a large bowl, coating with olive oil to prevent the pasta from sticking together. Chop all the ingredients into bite-sized pieces, but not too small since the beauty of the dish depends on the great variety of ingredients. Dress with approximately ¼ cup olive oil, basil, balsamic vinegar and salt and pepper and garlic to taste. Chill for several hours or overnight for flavors to mingle.

# Bleu Cheese Dressing

1 tablespoon dehydrated chopped onion
1 tablespoon fresh lemon juice
1 tablespoon tarragon vinegar
1 tablespoon garlic salt
1 tablespoon dried parsley
1 cup sour cream
1 pint mayonnaise
4 ounces bleu cheese, crumbled

Place dehydrated chopped onion in a medium glass bowl and barely cover with water. Allow to sit 10-15 minutes to reconstitute. Drain any unabsorbed water. Stir in lemon juice, vinegar, garlic salt, and dried parsley. Add sour cream, then mayonnaise, blending well. Stir in crumbled bleu cheese. Refrigerate at least 24 hours before using to allow flavors to develop. Keeps refrigerated for 2-3 weeks. Makes 4 cups

*Light or fat-free sour cream and mayonnaise will reduce fat and calories, with expected changes in flavor and consistency. Process in blender for an excellent dip for crackers or Buffalo hot wings.*

# Two Tomato Salsa

2 cups diced tomato
1 cup diced green tomato
½ cup diced green bell pepper
¼ cup diced purple onion
1 tablespoon seeded minced serrano chili
1 tablespoon chopped fresh cilantro
2 tablespoon fresh lime juice
1 tablespoon olive oil
1 teaspoon sugar
½ teaspoon salt
¼ teaspoon coarsely ground pepper
1 clove garlic, minced

Combine all ingredients in medium bowl, stir well. Cover and chill at least 3 hours. Serve with chicken or fish or as a dip with no oil baked tortilla chips. Makes 3½ cups

118

*Photo on right ~*
Belgian Asparagus Soup, page 99
*Herend Tureen*
*Courtesy Haltom's Jewelers*

# Poppy Seed Dressing

1½ cup sugar
1 tablespoon dry mustard
2 teaspoons vinegar
1 tablespoon onion juice
3 cups oil
3 tablespoons poppy seeds

Mix the first 4 ingredients in the blender on high. Gradually add the oil. Then mix in poppy seeds. 4½ cups

# Endive or Spinach Salad Dressing

½ cup vinegar
1 cup sugar
2 tablespoons cornstarch
cold water, enough to mix cornstarch
1 pound bacon, browned; reserve drippings
fresh mushrooms
endive or spinach (fresh)

Mix cornstarch with cold water. Add to bacon drippings. Add vinegar and sugar. Heat (microwave 2 minutes). Slice the bacon and mushrooms and put over the salad greens on individual plates. Pour hot dressing over salad just before serving. Makes 2 cups

# Raspberry Vinaigrette

¾ cup garlic, minced
6 cups olive oil
4 cups raspberry vinegar
½ cup Dijon mustard
¼ cup sugar

Mix well with wire whisk.

# Sesame Butter

½ pound butter, softened
3 tablespoons sesame seeds, toasted
2 green onions, sliced
1 tablespoon sesame oil
1 tablespoon soy sauce

Whip in mixer until all ingredients are thoroughly incorporated. Roll in parchment paper into a cylinder and chill.

*Photo on left ~*
Harvest of the Vine, page 19

# Papaya Relish

1     ripe papaya, peeled and cut into ¼ inch dice
1½   teaspoon seeded and finely chopped jalapeño pepper
¼    cup chopped red onion
¼    cup chopped green or red bell pepper
¼    cup fresh lime juice
     zest of 1 lime
1     tablespoon chopped fresh cilantro

Mix together and refrigerate 2-3 hours. Cover until time to use. Makes 2 cups

*Good with grilled chicken, pork or fish.*

# Béarnaise Sauce

3     tablespoons tarragon or cider vinegar
½    cup butter, melted
¼    cup water or dry white wine
3     tablespoons finely chopped onions or shallots
¼    teaspoon salt
3     egg yolks
½    cup mayonnaise
     pepper to taste

Combine all ingredients except mayonnaise in blender or food processor. Blend until ingredients are thoroughly mixed. Pour into pan or metal fondue pot. Cook, stirring until mixture thickens. Remove from heat and stir in mayonnaise. Serve with meat, fish or seafood fondue. Great over eggs. Makes 2 cups

Meats
and
Game

# Calzones (Quick and Easy)

1   (16 ounce) package ricotta cheese
1   (16 ounce) package cottage cheese, small curd
½   cup Parmesan cheese, grated or powdered, divided
½   cup Romano cheese, grated or powdered
8   ounces mozzarella cheese
1   pound Italian sausage, cooked
1   (10 ounce) package prepared pizza crust (or prepare as below)
1   jar prepared pizza sauce

Cream cheeses together. Cook for five minutes in microwave on medium high. Stir, and then cook for another 5 minutes, stirring once after 2½ minutes.

Put cheese filling on half of crust. Sprinkle with sausage. Fold other half over the top. Pinch sides together. Put on greased cookie sheet. Bake at 400 degrees for 10-12 minutes or until brown. Serve with hot pizza sauce and Parmesan cheese sprinkled on the top. Dough can be divided into individual servings.

## Pizza Crust

1   package dry yeast
1   cup warm water
2   tablespoons sugar
3   cups flour
2   teaspoons salt
2   tablespoons oil

Dissolve dry yeast and sugar in 1 cup warm water. Beat in ½ of the flour. Add salt, oil and remaining flour. Mix well. Knead in more flour until dough is not sticky. Place in an oiled bowl, turning dough to oil the top. Cover and let rise until doubled (about 1 hour) Divide dough in half. Pat to cover two cookie sheets and then cut each into 4 squares.

122

# Italian Beef on Hoagies

1 (3 pound) boneless beef round rump roast
1 (14½ ounce) can beef broth
½ cup water
6 cloves of garlic minced
2 teaspoons dried oregano, crushed
½ teaspoon crushed red pepper, or more to taste
¼ teaspoon black pepper
3 green sweet peppers, seeded and cut into strips
8 hoagie buns, split

Place roast, fat side up, on a rack in a shallow roasting pan. Roast, uncovered at 325 degrees for 1½ to 2 hours or to 145 degrees on a meat thermometer. (Do not overcook or meat will be tough.)

Transfer roast to a platter. Skim fat from the pan juices. Transfer juices to a covered container, chill. Cool roast 30 minutes. Cover, chill.

Using a very sharp knife, thinly slice the chilled roast across the grain. To serve, combine reserved meat juices, beef broth, water, garlic, oregano and red and black peppers in a 3 quart saucepan. Bring broth mixture to boiling; reduce heat. Add sliced meat and pepper strips. Simmer, uncovered 5 to 10 minutes. Spoon beef, peppers, and juices on buns. Serve remaining juices on the side. Serves 8

# Mexican Casserole

1½ pounds ground meat, browned (beef or turkey)
1 clove of garlic, chopped
1 can cream of mushroom soup
1 can cream of chicken soup
2 small cans taco sauce
1½ cups grated cheddar cheese
½ cup chopped onion
1 package corn tortillas

Simmer together browned meat, soups, sauces, and garlic over low heat for 15-20 minutes. Line a greased 9x13-inch casserole with tortillas. Layer with meat mixture, cheese, and onions (2 layers each) ending with cheese.

Bake at 350 degrees for 25-30 minutes. Cool 5 minutes before serving. Serves 6-8

123

# Uncle Bill's Deep Dish Pizza

Sauce

| | | |
|---|---|---|
| 1 | (8 ounce) can tomato paste | |
| 1 | can hot water | |
| 1 | teaspoon oregano, heaping | |
| ½ | teaspoon garlic salt, heaping | |
| ½ | teaspoon onion salt | |
| ½ | teaspoon lemon-pepper mix | |
| ½ | teaspoon black pepper | |
| ½ | teaspoon sugar | |
| 1 | small onion, minced or 1 tablespoon dried onion | |

Mix sauce ingredients and let stand while making the dough for the crust.

Crust

| | | |
|---|---|---|
| 1 | envelope rapid rise yeast | |
| 2 | cups water, 105 to 115 degrees in temperature | |
| 1 | tablespoon sugar | |
| 1 | tablespoon salt | |
| 5-6 | cups flour | |

Toppings

| | | |
|---|---|---|
| 1 | pound mozzarella cheese precooked ground beef, sausage, etc. | |

Place 1 cup of water in large mixing bowl. Sprinkle yeast over water then sprinkle 1 tablespoon sugar over that. Let "grow" for 5-10 minutes.

Add the other cup of water and 1 tablespoon of salt. Stir to blend and start adding flour 1 cup at a time to assure good mixture.

When dough starts to get too heavy or sticky, turn dough out on a floured surface and knead dough, adding flour until stickiness just begins to stop.

Return dough to the bowl and cover with a clean dish towel. Put in slightly warmed oven (oven off). Let rise for 45 minutes.

Turn dough out on a floured surface again and divide in half. Knead dough briefly to attain satin feel and to remove large air bubbles.

*(continued on next page)*

124

*(Uncle Bill's Deep Dish Pizza continued)*

Let dough rest another 20 minutes on counter, covered with towel. Spread dough on slightly oiled pan. Spread sauce on dough, cheese on sauce, toppings of choice.

Bake 25 minutes in a preheated oven at 425 degrees. Makes 2 12-inch pizzas

# Sloppy Joes

| | |
|---|---|
| 1 | pound lean ground beef (or ground turkey) |
| 1 | onion, chopped small |
| 1 | garlic clove, finely minced |
| 2 | tablespoons prepared mustard |
| 1 | tablespoon sugar, brown or white |
| 1 | tablespoon vinegar, any kind |
| 1 | teaspoon salt |
| 1 | cup catsup |
| 1 | bay leaf |
| 1 | red or green pepper, chopped (optional) |
| ¼ | teaspoon ground clove |

Brown beef. Drain off any fat and return to saucepan with onion and garlic. Cook, stirring occasionally until onion softens. Add other ingredients.

Turn heat to low and simmer, covered, stirring occasionally. Simmer for about one half hour.

Add a small amount of water if mixture seems too thick. Remove bay leaf.

Spoon onto split and toasted hamburger buns. Serves 4-6

# Sour Cream Chili Bake

1    pound ground beef, browned and drained
1    (15 ounce) can pinto beans, drained
1    (10 ounce) can hot enchilada sauce
1    (8 ounce) can tomato sauce
1½  cup shredded cheddar cheese
1    tablespoon minced onion
1    (6 ounce) package corn chips
1    cup sour cream

Combine browned ground beef, beans, enchilada sauce, tomato sauce, 1 cup of the shredded cheese, and the minced onion.

Set aside 1 cup of the corn chips; coarsely crush remaining chips. Stir crushed chips into meat mixture. Turn into a 1-½ quart casserole. Bake, covered, at 375 degrees for 30 minutes.

Spoon sour cream on top of casserole; sprinkle with the remaining ½ cup cheddar cheese. Sprinkle reserved chips around edge of casserole. Bake, uncovered, 2-3 minutes. Serves 6

# Sherried Tenderloin

1    (2 pound) beef tenderloin
2    tablespoons softened butter
¼  cup chopped green onion
¾  cup dry sherry
2    tablespoons soy sauce
1    teaspoon Dijon style mustard
    pinch coarsely ground pepper

Spread 1 tablespoon of butter over the meat. Place meat on a rack in a roasting pan. Roast, uncovered at 400 degrees for 20 minutes.

While tenderloin roasts, sauté onion in remaining 1 tablespoon of butter. Stir in sherry, soy sauce, mustard and pepper. Bring to a simmer. Pour over the meat and cook 20-25 minutes longer, basting frequently. Serve immediately. Pass the remaining sauce with the meat. Serves 4-6

# Marinated Châteaubriand

| | | |
|---|---|---|
| 3 | fresh jalapeño chili peppers | Halve peppers and remove stems, seed, and ribs. In a food processor combine jalapeños, wine, olive oil, garlic, parsley, salt and pepper. Process until smooth. Score surface of steak about ⅛ inch deep and 2 inches apart. Place in a large plastic bag and pour in marinade. Press out air and seal tightly. Massage bag to distribute marinade evenly. Refrigerate for at least 6 hours, turning and massaging bag occasionally. |
| ⅔ | cup dry red wine | |
| ⅓ | cup olive oil | |
| 2 | large cloves garlic | |
| 1 | handful of fresh parsley sprigs | |
| 1 | teaspoon salt | |
| ½ | teaspoon freshly ground pepper | |
| 1 | (3-4 pound) châteaubriand, at room temperature | |

Prepare low-fire grill. Position grill rack 4-6 inches from fire. Remove steak from bag and pat dry, reserving marinade. Grill meat 5 minutes per side, or until juices well up on surface for medium-rare. Remove from grill, rest meat for 10 minutes, and carve into thin slices on the diagonal and across the grain. Serves 4

# Garlic Roasted Châteaubriand

| | | |
|---|---|---|
| 2-2½ | pounds beef tenderloin | Preheat oven to 450 degrees. Cut ¾-inch deep slits in meat. Insert garlic into slits. Brush meat with oil. Heat remaining oil in skillet and brown meat on all sides. |
| 2 | large cloves garlic, slivered | |
| 2 | tablespoon olive oil | |

Set meat on roasting rack in a pan. Roast to desired doneness, approximately 30-40 minutes. If using a meat thermometer, 140 degrees for rare, 160 degrees for medium, and 170 for well done.

Serve with Béarnaise sauce or horseradish sauce. Serves 4-6

127

# Basil-Stuffed Beef

1    (3-3-½ pound) boneless beef sirloin roast, cut 1¾ inches thick
¼    teaspoon salt
¼    teaspoon black pepper
2    cups lightly packed basil leaves, snipped
8-10  cloves garlic, minced (2 tablespoons)
2    teaspoons olive oil

Make five or six 5-inch-long slits along the top of the roast, cutting almost through the roast. Sprinkle with salt and pepper.

For filling, in a medium bowl combine basil and garlic. Stuff the filling into the slits in the meat. Tie the meat with heavy-duty cotton string to hold the slits closed. Drizzle with olive oil.

Roast using indirect grilling, quick oven roasting, or slow oven roasting directions.

Indirect Grilling Directions: In a covered grill arrange medium coals around a drip pan. Test for medium-low heat above the pan. Place meat on grill rack over drip pan but not over the coals. Insert a meat thermometer, lower the grill hood. Grill for 45 minutes to 1-½ hours or till the meat thermometer registers the desired temperature (140 degrees for rare, 155 degrees for medium, 165 degrees for well done) Add more coals as necessary. Let meat stand, covered, for 10 minutes before slicing. (The meat temperature will rise slightly while standing.)

Slow Oven Roasting Directions: Place the roast on a rack in a shallow roasting pan. Insert a meat thermometer. Roast, uncovered, in a 325 degree oven for 1-½ to 1-¾ hours or until the meat thermometer registers 140 degrees or to desired doneness.

*(continued on next page)*

128

Let stand, covered for 10 minutes before slicing. (The meat temperature will rise slightly while standing.) Slice across the grain.

Quick Oven Roasting Directions: Place roast on a rack in a shallow roasting pan. Insert a meat thermometer. Roast, uncovered, in a 425 degree oven for 15 minutes. Reduce oven temperature to 350 degrees. Roast for 35 to 40 minutes more or till the thermometer registers 140 degrees or to a desired doneness. Let stand, covered, for 10 minutes before slicing, the temperature will rise slightly. Slice across the grain. Serves 10-12

# Barbecued Beef Brisket

⅓ cup molasses
⅓ cup prepared mustard
½ cup brown sugar, firmly packed
3 tablespoons Worcestershire sauce
¼ teaspoon hot pepper sauce
½ cup pineapple juice
1 teaspoon chili powder
¾ cup wine vinegar
1 tablespoon minced onions
6 pounds beef brisket

Combine all ingredients except beef, mixing well. Place meat in heavy plastic bag and pour marinade over it. Squeeze air from bag, and fasten bag. Place bag in a 13x9x2-inch baking dish. Marinate in refrigerator at least 4-6 hours, or overnight.

Drain meat and reserve marinade. Grill meat uncovered over medium heat until browned. Cover grill and cook 15 minutes longer.

Wrap meat in heavy foil, leaving room for marinade. Cut hole in top of foil and pour marinade through hole over the meat. Continue grilling for 2 hours or until meat is very tender.

To serve, slice thin diagonal slices.

# Spicy Beef Fillets with Black Bean Sauce

| | |
|---|---|
| 1 | onion |
| ½ | red bell pepper |
| ½ | green bell pepper |
| 2 | ears corn |
| 4 | (4 ounce) beef tenderloin steaks |
| ¼ | cup fajita seasoning |
| 1 | teaspoon olive oil, divided |
| 2 | cloves of garlic, minced |
| 1 | (15 ounce) can black beans, drained and rinsed |
| ¼ | cup chopped fresh cilantro |
| ½ | teaspoon salt |
| ½ | teaspoon black pepper |
| 2 | tablespoons fajita seasoning |
| ¼ | cup lime juice |

Cut onion and bell peppers into strips; cut corn from cob. Set aside.

Coat steaks with ¼ cup fajita seasoning. Heat ½ teaspoon oil in a heavy skillet; cook steaks in hot oil 2 to 3 minutes on each side or to desired degree of doneness. Keep warm.

Sauté onion, bell pepper, corn, and garlic in remaining ½ teaspoon oil until vegetables are crisp-tender. Stir in beans. Cook just until thoroughly heated. Add cilantro, salt, and pepper. Spoon half of mixture into a blender. Keep remaining mixture warm.

Add 2 tablespoons fajita seasoning and lime juice to blender. Process until smooth. Serve with steaks and remaining vegetable mixture. Serves 4

*Black bean sauce is awesome with any grilled beef.*

# Flank Steak on Skewers

| | |
|---|---|
| ⅓ | cup soy sauce (lite) |
| ⅓ | cup oil |
| 1 | package instant beef bouillon |
| 3 | tablespoons water |
| ½ | teaspoon ground ginger |
| ½ | garlic clove, minced (optional 1 or 2 cloves) |
| 1 | teaspoon parsley flakes |
| 1½ | pounds lean flank steak |
| 6 | (10 inch) bamboo skewers |

Cut flank steak (partially frozen) across grain into ⅛ inch to ¼ inch strips. Combine all other ingredients and marinate 1 to 2 hours or overnight. Skewer strips lengthwise and lightly salt and pepper. Broil 3 inches from flame, 4 minutes each side in broiler pan. May be placed on grill with slightly longer cooking time required. Serves 6

*Add ⅓ cup dry sherry or saki, 1 tablespoon sesame seeds, and 2 tablespoons chopped green onion to marinade mixture.*

# Beef Ragoût

| | |
|---|---|
| 3 | slices bacon, diced (reserve drippings) |
| 2 | pounds beef for stew or cubed steak(1½ inch cubes) |
| 1 | medium onion, sliced |
| 2 | cloves garlic, crushed |
| 1 | cup beef bouillon |
| 1 | cup red burgundy wine |
| 4 | medium carrots, thinly sliced (about 4 cups) |
| ½ | cup snipped parsley |
| 1 | small bay leaf |
| 1½ | teaspoons salt |
| ½ | teaspoon dried thyme |
| ½ | teaspoon dried savory leaves |
| ¼ | teaspoon freshly ground black pepper |
| ½ | pound mushrooms, quartered |
| ¼ | cup water |
| 3 | tablespoons flour |
| 8 | ounces noodles, cooked |

Cook bacon in Dutch oven until crisp. Remove bacon and set aside. Cook meat, onion, and garlic in bacon drippings until meat is brown and onion is tender. Stir often.

Add bacon, bouillon, wine, carrots, parsley, bay leaf, salt, pepper, thyme, and savory to meat mixture. Heat to boiling. Reduce heat and simmer until meat is tender, 1½-2 hours.

*Can be made to this point in advance. Cool slightly and cover. Refrigerate no longer than 48 hours. To serve; heat to boiling, then reduce and cook covered for about 15 minutes. Then finish recipe.*

Stir in mushrooms. Shake water and flour in tightly covered jar. Stir gradually into meat mixture. Heat to boiling, stirring constantly. Boil and stir one minute. Serve on cooked noodles. Serves 6

*Also works well in crock pot. The better the cut of beef, the more flavorful and tender the ragoût.*

# Filet Mignon with Mushroom Wine Sauce

3   teaspoons margarine, divided

    vegetable cooking spray

⅓   cup finely chopped shallots

½   pound fresh shiitake mushrooms, stems removed

1½ cups red wine (Cabernet Sauvignon) divided

1   (10½ ounce) can of undiluted beef consommé, divided

4   (4 ounce) filet mignon steaks, 1 inch thick

1   tablespoon low sodium soy sauce

2   teaspoons cornstarch

1   teaspoon dried thyme

1   bunch fresh thyme sprigs for garnish

Melt 1½ teaspoons margarine in nonstick skillet coated with non-stick spray over medium heat. Sauté shallots and mushrooms 4 minutes. Add 1 cup wine and ¾ cup consommé. Cook 5 minutes, stirring frequently. Remove mushrooms to a separate bowl, keeping warm. Increase heat to high and cook wine mixture 5-8 minutes until reduced to ½ cup. Add to mushrooms in bowl and set aside. Wipe skillet lightly with a paper towel.

Sprinkle pepper over steaks. Melt 1½ teaspoons margarine in skillet coated with cooking spray over medium heat. Cook steaks 3 minutes on each side or until browned. Reduce heat to medium-low and cook about 1-½ minutes on each side or until done to individual preference. Place on serving platter and keep warm.

Combine soy sauce and cornstarch in a bowl, stirring well. Add remaining wine and consommé to skillet, scraping with wooden spoon to loosen browned bits. Boil for 1 minute. Add mushroom mixture, cornstarch mixture, and 1 teaspoon dried thyme. Bring to a boil. Cook 1 minute, stirring constantly. Serve with steaks. Garnish with fresh thyme. Serves 4

# Marinated Flank Steak

1⅓ cups soy sauce
½ cup white wine (can use de-alcoholized)
4 teaspoons sugar (amount may be increased to 4 tablespoons if desired)
1 teaspoon ginger
2 cloves garlic, minced
8 chopped green onions
2 (2½ pound) flank steaks

Mix soy sauce, white wine, sugar, ginger, garlic, and green onions together in a large reclosable plastic bag. Puncture the steak with a fork several times. Add the flank steaks to the zip top bag and marinate in refrigerator for 24 hours, turning over several times.

Grill on both sides for 6 minutes for medium rare, or to desired doneness. Serve with bleu cheese sauce or steak marinade sauce. Serves 8

*Chicken breasts may be substituted for flank steak.*

## Bleu Cheese Sauce
½ cup butter
1 cup blue cheese, crumbled
2 cloves of garlic, minced
2 tablespoons chives, chopped
4 tablespoons brandy or wine

Heat together and serve warm over thin slices of steak.

## Steak Marinade Sauce
After marinating steaks for 24 hours, reserve marinade and set aside. While steaks are being grilled, place marinade in a heavy saucepan and add ¼ cup red wine. Bring to a rapid boil and reduce sauce by ⅓ to ½. Sauce should be thick and rich in texture. If sauce appears a little watery, thicken by adding small amounts of cornstarch dissolved in a small amount of water.

# Veal Piccata

1 pound veal, sliced thin
¼ cup flour
½ teaspoon salt
⅛ teaspoon black pepper
1 tablespoon vegetable oil
1½ tablespoons butter
½ pound sliced mushrooms
3 tablespoons white wine
1 tablespoon lemon juice

Gently pound the veal into very thin pieces about 8 inches in diameter. Mix flour, salt and pepper. Lightly flour veal. Melt oil and butter in 10 inch frying pan. Sauté veal until golden brown on medium heat. Cook about 3 minutes on each side. Remove veal and keep warm. Cook mushrooms in frying pan for several minutes. Add wine and lemon juice. Boil rapidly to reduce sauce slightly. Pour over veal to serve. Serves 4

*Use chicken breasts instead of veal.*


# Pork Chile Verde

1 pound pork tenderloin, cut in ½-inch cubes
1 medium onion, chopped
1 large green bell pepper, chopped
1 tablespoon olive oil
1 small fresh jalapeño pepper, seeded, deveined and diced
1½ teaspoons ground cumin
1 teaspoon chili powder
2 cloves garlic minced
½ teaspoon crushed dried red chile pepper
1 (16 ounce) can chicken broth
salt and pepper to taste
4 servings of cooked rice

Sauté pork, onion and green bell pepper in olive oil until the pork is cooked through. Add jalapeño, chili powder, garlic, red pepper, chicken broth, salt and pepper and simmer 1 hour.

Serve over rice. Serves 4

*This freezes well. Can be topped with sour cream, cheese, red onions or tomatoes. Also delicious inside a flour tortilla as a burrito.*

# Sherried Pork Chops

6    ½-¾-inch thick pork
      chops
      salt and pepper to taste
¼    cup flour
3-4   tablespoons olive oil
⅓    cup water
⅔    cup chopped green onion
½    pound fresh sliced mush-
      rooms
⅔    cup sherry

Salt and pepper chops to taste. Dust lightly with flour and brown in oil. Arrange chops in casserole pan. Cover with mushrooms, onions, sherry and water. Cook at 350 degrees for 35-45 minutes. Sauce can be used as gravy over chops or rice. Serves 4-6

# Chinese Marinated Pork

¼    cup soy sauce
2    tablespoons honey
2    tablespoons sugar
2    tablespoons dry sherry
1    teaspoon salt
1    teaspoon Chinese five-
      spice
3    slices fresh ginger root,
      quarter size, crushed
      with side of cleaver
3    pounds pork tenderloin

In a pan combine soy sauce, honey, sugar, dry sherry, salt, five-spice and ginger. Heat for 1 minute to dissolve sugar; cool.

Cut meat in 2-inch thick slices and place in a plastic bag. Pour cooled marinade over meat, then seal and refrigerate for 4 hours or overnight. Turn bag occasionally to distribute the marinade. Remove meat from marinade and place on a rack set over a foil lined baking pan. Reserve marinade.

Bake in a 350 degree oven for 30 minutes. Turn pieces over and continue baking for 45 minutes, brushing occasionally with reserved marinade. Cut in thin slices and serve hot or cold. Serves 10 as an appetizer.

*Also called "char siu," barbecued pork can be used many ways. The Chinese serve it as an appetizer and as a garnish for fried rice, wonton soup, noodles, or stir-fried vegetables.*

# Chinese Barbecued Pork

½ cup soy sauce
¼ cup granulated sugar
½ teaspoon garlic powder
1 tablespoon catsup
¼ teaspoon salt
1 tablespoon Hoi Sin sauce
  or catsup
1 pound pork tenderloin

Marinate pork for at least 3 hours in sauce, turning frequently. Drain pork and roast on rack for 40 minutes at 350 degrees, turning every 10 minutes to assure even browning. Slice ¼ inch thick. Makes about 25 slices depending on meat size.

*May be sprinkled with toasted sesame seeds. Hot mustard or soy sauce dip optional*

# Herbed Pork Pinwheels

3 small sweet red or yellow peppers, finely chopped
¾ cup finely chopped onion
¾ cup finely chopped celery
1½ teaspoons dried whole thyme, crushed
¾ teaspoon garlic salt
⅛ teaspoon crushed red pepper (or more to suit your taste)
¾ teaspoon paprika
3 tablespoons vegetable oil
3 pork tenderloins (¾ pound each)
1½ tablespoons fennel seeds, crushed
1 tablespoon lemon-pepper seasoning (or more to suit your taste)

Sauté sweet peppers, onion, celery and thyme until tender. Add salt, red pepper, and paprika, set aside. Slice each tenderloin lengthwise down center cutting to, but not through, bottom. Place each between sheets of heavy duty plastic wrap. Using a meat mallet, pound to a 12x8-inch rectangle of even thickness.

Spoon ⅓ of sweet pepper mixture onto tenderloin, spreading to within ½ inch of sides. Roll tenderloin jelly roll fashion starting with short side. Tie with heavy string at 1½ inch intervals. Repeat with remaining 2 tenderloins and sweet pepper mixture. Combine fennel seeds and lemon pepper seasoning. Rub on top and sides of tenderloins. Place seam side down on lightly greased rack in a shallow pan. Bake uncovered at 350 degrees for 45 minutes or until done. Let stand 10 minutes. Remove strings and slice. Serves 10

# Medallions of Pork Tenderloin Véronique

1    (3 pound) pork tenderloin, cut
½    teaspoon salt
⅓    teaspoon white pepper
6    tablespoons unsalted butter
2    ounces shallots, chopped
1    cup beef broth
½    cup sherry wine
½    cup heavy cream (may use half-and-half or skimmed evaporated)
½    pound seedless grapes
     parsley to garnish

Cut pork tenderloin in 3-ounce portions. Season with salt and white pepper and sauté in butter. Remove from pan and set aside while keeping hot. In the same pan, add more butter and sauté chopped shallots for 2 minutes.

Deglaze with sherry and broth. Bring to a boil, scraping the bottom of the pan to dissolve all the drippings from the tenderloin. Reduce to half volume.

Add heavy cream, reduce sauce and adjust seasoning. Add tenderloin to sauce. If the sauce is a little thin, thicken with cornstarch.

Sauté seedless grapes in butter. Place 2 tenderloin fillets on a dinner plate with 4-5 grapes on top. Then spoon sauce over meat. Garnish with parsley. Serves 8

# Marinated Pork Tenderloin with Jicama Salsa

| | |
|---|---|
| 1 | pork tenderloin |
| 2 | large lemons, zest of one removed and cut into strips. |
| ¼ | cup rosemary leaves |
| 3 | large cloves garlic, finely minced |
| ½ | large onion, finely minced |
| 3 | tablespoons extra virgin olive oil (good grade), divided |
| ½ | cup lemon juice |
| ½ | teaspoon salt |
| 1½ | tablespoons coarsely ground black pepper |
| 1½ | cups water |
| 1 | bouquet garni composed of 5 fresh parsley sprigs, 3 fresh thyme sprigs, and 2 bay leaves tied in cheese cloth. |

Preheat oven to 350 degrees. Cut off and discard pith from zested lemon. In a saucepan of boiling water blanch zest 1 minute and drain in colander. Cut each lemon crosswise into 6 slices.

In a small food processor blend rosemary, garlic, zest, 2 tablespoons olive oil, lemon juice and salt until mixture is chopped fine. With the tip of a knife cut a few small slits into the pork and rub marinade mixture all over tenderloin and into slits. Arrange lemon slices in middle of a large roasting pan and place tenderloin on them. Roast tenderloin in oven for 1 hour.

In a small saucepan add bouquet garni to 1½ cups water. Cook slowly over low heat. After tenderloin has cooked for about an hour remove from oven and gently and slowly pour aromatic water around the edges of the roasting pan, being careful not to get any on the top of the tenderloin which has started to brown at this point. Discard garni. Return to oven and finish roasting until desired doneness.

When cooked, remove from oven and allow to rest before you slice thinly across the grain. Serve with jicama salsa.

*(continued on next page)*

138

Jicama Salsa

| | |
|---|---|
| 1 | large jicama |
| 1 | fresh pineapple |
| 1 | bunch fresh cilantro |
| 1 | small fresh jalapeño, if desired |

Peel and core pineapple, reserving as much fresh pineapple juice as possible. Dice pineapple into a large bowl.

Peel jicama. Slice into julienne strips or chop. Add to the diced pineapple. Wash and dry cilantro. Chop and add ⅔ cup to bowl. Fresh Cilantro is strong and may overpower the salsa. Add more to taste if needed after completion. Wash and finely chop the jalapeño and add to salsa.

*The contributor likes to serve this to visitors from out of state. They often think Tex-Mex is only enchiladas and many have a difficult time guessing what the "crunch" is in the salsa. The jicama is rather bland and takes on the taste of what it is served with, so that is why she likes to serve it with pineapple. Also the sweet taste of the pineapple with the hotter taste of jalapeño and cilantro make a nice accompaniment. Make the salsa as hot or as tame as you like.*

# Venison Pie with Currant Jelly

1   2-inch thick cut boned top round venison (1 pound) beaten with mallet until tender
2   cups flour
2   eggs, beaten
½   tablespoon salt
½   cup water
6   slices bacon
    salt and pepper to taste

Combine flour, eggs, salt, and water to make a pastry shell.

Preheat oven to 425 degrees.

Roll out pastry until thin on floured surface. Place on a baking sheet lined with heavy duty aluminum foil. Arrange bacon slices on top of pastry. Put the venison on top of the bacon. Moisten edges of pastry and draw around meat and pinch together the edges. To seal, wrap this "pie" in the heavy aluminum foil.

Place on baking sheet and cook 50 minutes per pound. 15 minutes before meat is due to be done, open foil and increase heat to 450 degrees and bake to brown and steaming. Serve with currant jelly. Serves 4-6

*A garden salad is a good side dish.*

140

# Moussaka

| | |
|---|---|
| 1 | large eggplant |
| ½ | teaspoon salt, or to taste |
| 1 | pound ground lamb |
| 1 | onion chopped |
| 2 | garlic cloves, minced |
| ½ | teaspoons dried thyme |
| ½ | teaspoon oregano |
| ¼ | teaspoon nutmeg |
| 2 | tablespoons parsley |
| 1 | cup canned tomatoes |
| ½ | cup white wine |
| 2 | egg whites |
| ½ | cup commercial bread crumbs |

Cut eggplant into ½ inch slices. Sprinkle with ½ teaspoon salt. Allow to ripen for ½ hour. Meanwhile, brown ground lamb with onion and garlic. Drain off fat. Add thyme, oregano, nutmeg. parsley, tomatoes and wine. Cover and cook slowly for thirty minutes. Cool.

Mix unbeaten egg whites and half the crumbs. In olive oil, brown dried eggplant slices coated in egg crumb mixture. Sprinkle remaining bread crumbs on bottom of 9x12-inch glass casserole dish. Cover with layer of eggplant. Spoon meat mixture on top. Pour sauce over all. Bake at 350 degrees for 45 minutes.

## Sauce Recipe

| | |
|---|---|
| 3 | tablespoons flour |
| 3 | tablespoons butter |
| 1½ | cups milk |
| ½ | teaspoon salt |
| 2 | egg yolks |
| 4 | tablespoons grated Parmesan cheese |
| | salt and pepper to taste |

Melt butter. Add flour and mix well. Add milk slowly and stir as it thickens. Slowly add beaten egg yolks, salt and pepper, stirring constantly.

*Entire recipe may be made one day ahead.*

# Savory Rabbit Provençal

*Marinated rabbit cooked in an anchovy and garlic sauce*

| | |
|---|---|
| 6 | fresh rabbit breasts |
| 6 | fresh rabbit thighs |
| 5 | tablespoons olive oil |
| 1 | teaspoon rosemary |
| 5 | garlic cloves, divided |
| 2 | bay leaves |
| 3 | teaspoons thyme |
| 3 | small onions, chopped |
| 10 | peppercorns |
| 2 | cups dry white wine |
| 4 | chicken livers |
| 8 | anchovy fillets chopped |
| 1 | bunch parsley divided |
| 2 | tablespoons capers |
| ½ | cup black pitted oil cured olives |
| 1 | cup croutons |
| ½ | cup flour for dredging |

The night before you plan to serve, place the rabbit in a large bowl. Sprinkle with 3 tablespoons olive oil and rosemary. Peel and crush 2 cloves of garlic and spread on meat. Add bay leaves. Cover dish and leave overnight in the refrigerator.

The next day remove meat from marinade and sprinkle with 1 teaspoon of thyme. Heat marinade in a heavy bottomed pan on medium heat. Add rabbit and sauté for 10 minutes. Remove rabbit from pan and place on a plate. Add onions to pan and sauté for 5 minutes, once again add meat to pan with 2 teaspoons of thyme, peppercorns, and 2 cups wine. Simmer ingredients uncovered for 30 minutes until meat is tender. There should be about 1 cup of juice left in pan. Put the meat and juices aside in a bowl. Do not wash the large cooking pan.

Dredge the chicken livers in flour. Heat 2 tablespoons olive oil in a small frying pan. Add chicken livers and sauté for 3 minutes. In a blender puree the sautéed livers, anchovies and 3 peeled garlic cloves for 2 minutes. Stir into this mixture the parsley, capers, and olives.

Return the rabbit and juices to the large pan. Slowly add the thick puree to the pan, covering all the meat evenly. Allow this dish to rest for about an hour on the counter before the final heating.

*(continued on next page)*

142

This is the time to prepare a salad and/or side dish. About 20 minutes before you wish to serve dinner simmer slowly in the uncovered pan.

To serve, warm your platter. Put rabbit in the center. Pour the sauce over the meat. Garnish with parsley and spread croutons along the sides of the dish. Serves 6

*This is excellent with a dry white wine. Chicken may be substituted for rabbit. The evening before the dish is to be served, clean and prepare marinade ingredients. The day the dish is to be prepared, have fresh ingredients ready to add to mixture.*

# Tom's Grilled Marinated Leg of Lamb

6  pound leg of lamb
1  cup olive oil
¼  cup lemon juice
2  cloves garlic, slivered
2  tablespoons fresh rosemary

Have butcher bone and butterfly lamb, or do it yourself. Place in a shallow glass, stainless-steel, or hard plastic pan to marinate.

In a small bowl, combine olive oil, lemon juice, garlic and rosemary. Pour mixture over lamb, spreading garlic slivers evenly. Marinate for 1 hour at room temperature. If preparing to cook later or the next day, lamb should be covered and refrigerated. Prepare and light the grill. Grill lamb when coals are searing hot and gray in color. Grill, turning and basting with marinade, until as well done as you prefer. For optimum taste, a juicy medium-rare is the best choice. Cook for 20-35 minutes.

143

# Lamb Shrewsbury

3 pounds lamb from shoulder or leg, trimmed of all fat and cut into small bite-size chunks

3 tablespoons vegetable oil

½ pound sliced fresh mushrooms

2 tablespoons corn starch

½ cup red currant jelly

4 teaspoons Worcestershire sauce

1 fresh lemon, juiced

2 cups beef stock

2 pinches ground nutmeg

3 tablespoons chopped fresh parsley

¼ teaspoon black pepper, or to taste

Heat oil in large frying pan and brown lamb on all sides. Transfer to casserole with slotted spoon. Cover with sliced mushrooms

Dissolve cornstarch in a little of the pan juices and put in frying pan with black pepper, nutmeg, lemon juice, beef stock, Worcestershire, parsley and currant jelly.

Cook and stir until ingredients have turned into gravy which is then poured over meat and mushrooms in casserole. Cover casserole and bake at 325 degrees for 2 hours. Serves 8

*Dinner party entrée, especially good with steamed new potatoes or baked sweet potatoes. May be prepared ahead and freezes well.*

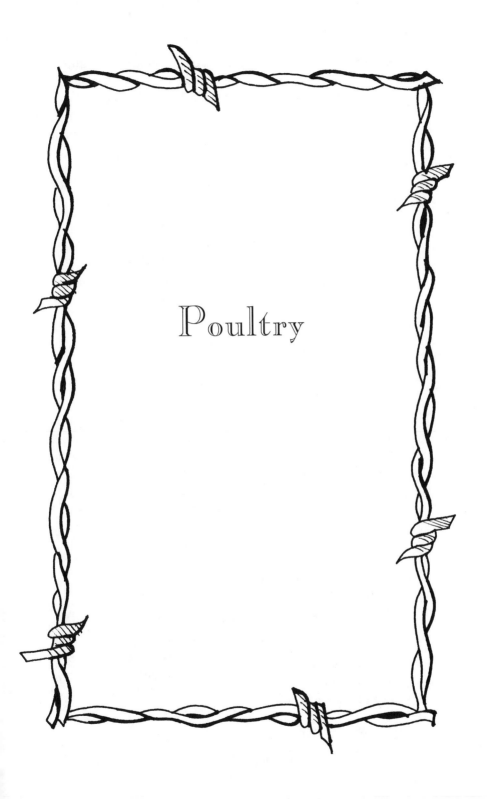

Poultry

# Sesame Baked Chicken

8 skinned chicken breasts
¾ cup buttermilk
2 tablespoons freshly
   squeezed lemon juice
3 cloves garlic, minced
¾ cup melted butter
Bread Crumb Mixture
1½ cups bread crumbs
½ cup sesame seed
½ teaspoon salt
½ teaspoon pepper
2 tablespoons Parmesan
   cheese

Soak chicken breasts in buttermilk overnight. Next day dry chicken on a paper towel. Dip dry chicken in melted butter, lemon juice and garlic. Roll each piece of chicken in bread crumb mixture and place in a 9x13-inch pan and cook at 450 degrees for 10 minutes, then reduce to 350 degrees for 1 hour. Serves 8

*Reduce cooking time by cutting chicken into bite-sized pieces and cooking at 450 degrees for 10 minutes, then reduce to 350 degrees for 30 minutes.*

# Mexican Chicken Mole

1 chicken, cut up
¼ cup olive oil
½ minced onion
4 garlic cloves, minced
2 (8 ounce) cans tomato
   sauce
¾ ounce unsweetened
   chocolate
1½ tablespoons peanut butter
2 tablespoons sesame seeds
   (optional)
3 tablespoons sliced al-
   monds (optional)
1½ teaspoons chili powder
   pinch of cloves
   pinch cinnamon
   salt and pepper to taste

Brown chicken in olive oil. Remove and set aside. Sauté onion and garlic, add remaining ingredients to make sauce. Balance the taste between the chocolate and peanut butter. (Peanut butter makes it sweet, chocolate makes it bitter). Add chicken back to sauce and simmer 1 hour. Serve with Mexican rice and a side salad. Serves 4

*Variation: for almond crusted mole: Mix ½ cup almonds lightly chopped with 1 teaspoon black sesame seeds. Dip chicken in water and roll in almonds and sesame seeds. Brown lightly in oil and bake in oven for 20 minutes at 350 degrees. Serve on top of mole sauce*

146

# Cornish Hens with Fruit Stuffing

4  1 pound frozen or fresh Cornish hens

   salt

**Glaze**

1  cup apricot nectar

2  tablespoons apricot jam

½  teaspoon grated orange peel

2  tablespoons brown sugar

4  whole cloves

4  tablespoons dry white wine

1  tablespoon cornstarch

**Fruit Stuffing**

2  cups coarsely cut packaged mixed dried fruits

¼  teaspoon rosemary leaves

¼  teaspoon thyme leaves

¼  teaspoon basil leaves

½  teaspoon salt

½  cup chopped pecans

4  tablespoons melted butter

Heat oven to 350 degrees. Clean hens and salt insides lightly. Combine nectar, jam, orange peel, brown sugar and cloves in a small saucepan. Bring to a boil over moderate heat. In a small bowl combine the wine and cornstarch and stir into hot mixture. Cook, stirring frequently, until mixture is thickened and smooth. Remove from heat.

Combine the stuffing ingredients in a small bowl, add 2 tablespoons of the hot glaze mixture and stuff the hens with fruit stuffing. Fasten skin over opening with small skewers. Place hens in baking pan and baste with glaze. Roast 1-1½ hours, or until leg joints move freely. Baste frequently with glaze. Serve on white or wild rice. Serves 4

# Mexican Lasagna

½  bag of tortillas chips

4  boneless, skinless chicken breasts, cooked and shredded

1  (10¾ ounce) can condensed cream of chicken soup

1  can diced tomatoes with chilies or picante sauce

1  small onion, minced

1½  cups shredded cheddar cheese or Monterey Jack cheese

Spray a 9x13-inch pan with nonstick cooking spray. Layer tortillas on bottom of pan (Just enough chips to make one good solid layer). Then layer all the shredded chicken on top of tortillas. In another bowl, mix soup, tomatoes and onion. Pour over chicken and tortilla chips. Top with the shredded cheddar. Bake at 350 degrees for 35-45 minutes. Serves 4-6

*May substitute ground meat for chicken*

# Chicken Wellington with Port-Currant Sauce

| | |
|---|---|
| 2 | tablespoons unsalted butter |
| 12 | ounces fresh, clean mushrooms, minced |
| 1 | medium onion, peeled and minced |
| 2 | garlic cloves, peeled and crushed |
| 2-3 | gratings fresh nutmeg |
| ¼ | teaspoon dried thyme, crushed |
| ½ | teaspoon dried leaf basil, crushed |
| | salt and pepper to taste |
| 3 | tablespoons Madeira wine |
| 1 | package (17½ ounce) frozen puff pastry, thawed |
| 2 | whole chicken breasts (4 conventional breast pieces) boned and skinned |
| 1 | large egg |
| 2 | tablespoons water |
| 1 | (10 ounce) jar red currant jelly |
| 1 | tablespoon prepared mustard |
| 3 | tablespoons port wine |
| ¼ | cup lemon juice |

Duxelles: In 12 inch skillet melt butter over medium high heat. When butter sizzles add mushrooms, onion and garlic. Sauté stirring occasionally, until all moisture given up by mushrooms and onion evaporates, 10-15 minutes. Stir in nutmeg, thyme, basil, salt and pepper to taste, add Madeira. Sauté another 2 minutes. Remove from heat. Cool.

Duxelles can be made, covered and refrigerated up to 24 hours ahead of assembling Wellingtons.

Wellingtons: Lay one sheet of thawed puff pastry on lightly floured board. Roll to 12-inch square. Cut pastry into 4 equal 6-inch squares. Set aside on counter. Repeat with other sheet of puff pastry. Divide Duxelles equally among 8 squares of pastry, placing mixture in center of each and flattening slightly. Skin, bone, split and pat dry chicken. Using 4 breast pieces from 2 chickens, halve each breast, resulting in 8 pieces of chicken. Top each portion of duxelles with 1 piece of chicken. Season with salt and freshly ground black pepper. Bring sides of pastry around chicken, pinching pastry edges together to enclose chicken. Place pastry wrapped chicken, seam side down on foil lined baking sheet. Recipe can be made to this point 6 hours before baking. Cover tightly with foil, refrigerate.

*(continued on next page)*

Preheat oven to 350 degrees. In small bowl lightly beat egg with water. Brush each Wellington with egg mixture using a pastry brush. Take care not to drip excess egg on baking sheet or Wellingtons will stick to foil. Bake uncovered at 350 degrees 45-55 minutes or until Wellingtons are golden brown.

While Wellingtons are baking, make Port-Currant Sauce by mixing currant jelly, mustard, wine and lemon juice in saucepan. Heat. Serve sauce warm in sauce boat. Arrange Wellingtons on an attractive platter and garnish with parsley and cherry tomatoes. Serves 8

# Turkey Noodle Casserole

| | |
|---|---|
| 1 | package, medium egg noodles |
| ½ | cup chopped onions |
| ¼ | cup diced green pepper |
| ¼ | cup margarine |
| 3 | tablespoons flour |
| 3 | cups milk |
| ¼ | cup grated Parmesan cheese |
| 1 | tablespoon poppy seeds |
| 1 | teaspoon salt |
| ⅛ | teaspoon cayenne pepper |
| 1 | (4 ounce) jar diced pimento |
| 3 | cups cooked cubed turkey |
| 2 | tablespoons Parmesan cheese |

Cook noodles. Drain and set aside. Sauté onion and green pepper in melted margarine. Add flour and cook 1 minute. Gradually add milk, stirring until thickened. Add ¼ cup Parmesan cheese. Pour sauce over noodles. Add poppy seeds, salt, cayenne pepper, pimento and turkey. Mix well. Spoon into 9x12-inch greased baking dish. Cover and chill 8 hours or overnight.

To bake, remove from refrigerator and let stand 30 minutes. Bake covered at 350 degrees for 30 minutes. Uncover, sprinkle with 2 tablespoons Parmesan. Bake 10 minutes longer. Serves 8

*Chicken may be used instead of turkey.*

# Chicken Bundles

1  (3 ounce) package cream cheese, softened
3  tablespoons margarine, melted and divided
¼  teaspoon salt
¼  teaspoon black pepper
2  tablespoons milk
1  tablespoon chopped green onions
2  cups chicken or turkey
1  (8 ounce) can refrigerated crescent rolls
¾  cup Italian bread crumbs

Mix cream cheese and 2 tablespoons margarine together in a bowl. Add salt, pepper, milk, green onions, and chicken. Mix well. Separate crescent rolls into 4 rectangles, pressing seam together or overlap seam to make strong bond. Put a fourth of the mixture in the middle of each rectangle. Pull 4 corners of each rectangle to the center, twisting slightly together at the top. Brush with remaining margarine, sprinkling bread crumbs on top.

Place on baking sheet and bake at 350 degrees for 20-25 minutes. Serves 4

# Hot Chicken Party Casserole

6  pounds chicken breasts, cooked and cubed
1  cup slivered almonds
1  (8 ounce) can water chestnuts, drained and sliced
1  (2 ounce) jar diced pimentos
1  cup celery, diced
8  ounces cheddar cheese, grated
1  cup milk
3  cups mayonnaise
   juice of one lemon
1  (5 ounce) can chow mein noodles, crushed

Toss together all ingredients except the chow mein noodles. Pour into two 8x11-inch greased glass casserole dishes. Top with crushed noodles. Bake at 350 degrees for 25-30 minutes. Serves 16

*Can be assembled except for noodles the day before and refrigerated.*

*Photo on right ~*
Cantrell Chili, page 92
and Blue Corn Muffins, page 74

150

# Skillet Chicken Tetrazzini

| | |
|---|---|
| 3 | tablespoons butter |
| 1 | medium onion, chopped |
| 1 | stalk celery, chopped |
| 2 | cups cooked chicken, cut into strips |
| 6 | ounces uncooked vermicelli or spaghetti |
| 1 | teaspoon salt |
| ¼ | teaspoon pepper |
| 1 | can condensed cream of chicken soup |
| 1½ | cups chicken broth or bouillon |
| 1 | (¾ ounce) can sliced mushrooms |
| ½ | cup grated Parmesan cheese |
| | paprika |

Melt butter in large skillet. Add onion and celery, cook until clear. Arrange chicken in layer, add spaghetti. Mix salt, pepper, cream of chicken soup, and broth or bouillon. Pour over spaghetti, carefully moistening all spaghetti. Place mushrooms over top. Sprinkle with Parmesan cheese and paprika. Cover and cook over high until steam escapes. Turn immediately to simmer and cook 30 minutes.

*Substitute leftover turkey for chicken.*

# Saucy Cranberry Chicken

| | |
|---|---|
| 4 | whole chicken breasts |
| 2 | teaspoons seasoned flavor enhancer, divided |
| ½ | cup flour |
| ¼ | cup cracker meal |
| ¼ | teaspoon salt |
| ⅛ | teaspoon pepper |
| ⅛ | teaspoon paprika |
| ½ | cup corn oil |
| 1 | (16 ounce) can jellied cranberry sauce |
| 1 | (12 ounce) bottle chili sauce |
| 1 | tablespoon brown sugar |
| 1 | tablespoon lemon juice |

Sprinkle chicken with 1 teaspoon flavor enhancer. Let stand 10 minutes. Mix together remaining flavor enhancer, flour, cracker meal, salt, pepper, and paprika. Roll chicken in mixture.

Brown chicken in oil, then place browned chicken in large glass casserole dish.

In sauce pan mix cranberry sauce, chili sauce, brown sugar, and lemon juice. Cook over medium heat, stirring constantly until cranberry sauce is melted and smooth. Spoon over chicken. Bake uncovered at 350 degrees about 45 minutes to until tender. Serves 4

*Photo on left ~*
Armadillo Hunt Brunch,
page 11

151

# Cherry Pepper Chicken

| | |
|---|---|
| 2 | pounds boneless, skinless chicken breast, cut into bite size pieces |
| 2 | tablespoons olive oil |
| 1 | medium onion, chopped |
| 3 | cloves garlic, chopped |
| 10 | pickled cherry peppers |
| 1½ | ounces dried yellow tomatoes or dried red tomatoes |
| 1½ | cups white wine |
| 2 | tablespoons dried tarragon |
| 1 | teaspoon salt |
| ½ | teaspoon black pepper |
| 1 | tablespoon sugar |

Sauté chicken in oil until browned. Drain on paper towels and keep warm. In oil sauté onion and garlic, until limp. Add cherry peppers, tomatoes, wine, tarragon, salt, pepper and sugar. Add chicken, simmer until sauce is reduced, about 15 minutes. Serves 4

# Jamaican Jerk Chicken

| | |
|---|---|
| ⅔ | cup chopped green onion |
| 3 | tablespoons fresh thyme or 1 tablespoon dried thyme |
| 3 | tablespoons peanut oil |
| 3 | tablespoons soy sauce |
| 2 | tablespoons minced fresh ginger |
| 1 | tablespoon garlic, minced |
| 4 | shakes cayenne pepper |
| 1 | bay leaf |
| 1 | teaspoon ground coriander |
| 1 | teaspoon ground black pepper |
| ⅓ | teaspoon ground nutmeg |
| ½ | teaspoon ground allspice |
| 4 | chicken breast halves, boned and skinned |

Combine all ingredients except chicken mixing to blend well. Coat chicken with mixture. Marinate in covered container in refrigerator, several hours or overnight. Grill on covered grill over medium coals, 4 to 6 minutes on each side until cooked through. Serves 4

*May substitute chicken with pork tenderloin.*

# Curried Chicken Delight

| | | |
|---|---|---|
| 2 | boneless, skinless chicken breasts | |
| 1 | teaspoon curry powder | |
| 2 | stalks crisp celery, chopped | |
| ¼ | cup walnuts or pecans, chopped | |
| ½ | teaspoon freshly grated pepper | |
| | salt to taste | |
| 2 | tablespoons mayonnaise | |
| 4 | puff pastry cups, cooked and cooled | |
| | cranberry relish | |

Cook chicken until tender. When cool, place in large bowl and break with fork. Add curry powder, celery, walnuts, pepper and salt. When well blended add mayonnaise, using only enough to bind mixture together. Place in cooked puff pastry cup that has been cooked and cooled. Top with cranberry relish. Serves 4

# Chicken Florentine

| | |
|---|---|
| 3 | chicken breasts, boned and skinned |
| | salt to taste |
| | pepper to taste |
| 2 | tablespoons butter, melted |
| 1 | (3 ounce) package cream cheese |
| 1 | teaspoon oregano |
| 1 | tablespoon lemon juice |
| 1 | bunch fresh spinach, cooked, drained, and chopped |
| ½ | cup shredded Swiss cheese |
| 6 | tablespoons butter, unmelted, divided |
| ½ | cup grated Parmesan cheese |

Preheat oven to 400 degrees.

Pound chicken until thin. Season with salt and pepper, set aside.

Mix melted butter, cream cheese, oregano, and lemon juice with spinach in large bowl. In center of each breast, spread Swiss cheese and ¼ cup of spinach mixture.

Fold chicken to cover stuffing completely. Place in baking dish, seam side down, and place ½ table-spoon butter on each chicken breast. Sprinkle Parmesan cheese on each chicken breast. Add remaining butter and small amount of water. Bake 20 minutes at 400 degrees until browned. Serves 6 to 8

# Chicken with Irish Whiskey and Cream Sauce

Cream Sauce

| | | |
|---|---|---|
| 2 | tablespoons butter or margarine | Melt butter in a heavy non-aluminum sauce pan over medium heat. Add mushrooms, shallots, garlic, salt and pepper. Cook until vegetables are soft, stirring occasionally, 10 minutes. Add wine and simmer 5 minutes. Add all remaining ingredients. Boil over medium heat until reduced by half, 40 minutes. |
| ¼ | pound mushrooms, finely chopped | |
| 4 | medium shallots, finally chopped | |
| 1 | medium garlic clove, minced | |
| | pinch of salt | |
| | freshly ground pepper | |
| ½ | cup dry white wine | |
| 2 | cups chicken stock | |
| 1 | cup whipping cream | |
| ½ | teaspoon paprika | |
| | pinch of nutmeg | |
| | pinch of ground sage | |

Chicken

| | | |
|---|---|---|
| 4 | pound chicken, quartered and backbone discarded | Pat chicken dry. Sprinkle with lemon juice. Mix salt, pepper, paprika and thyme in small bowl. Rub all over chicken. Heat butter in heavy 12 inch skillet over medium high heat. Add chicken, skin side down, and brown, 5 minutes. Turn and cook 5 minutes longer. |
| 3 | tablespoons fresh lemon juice | |
| 1 | teaspoon salt | |
| 1 | teaspoon freshly ground pepper | |
| ½ | teaspoon paprika | |
| ½ | teaspoon dried thyme, crumbled | Reduce heat to low and add whiskey. Ignite with match. Shake pan until flame subsides. Cover pan and simmer until chicken is tender, 20 to 25 minutes. |
| 3 | tablespoons butter or margarine | |
| ¼ | cup Irish whiskey | |

Transfer chicken to plate. Degrease pan juices. Strain in cream sauce. Simmer until thickened and reduced to consistency of whipping cream, 15 minutes. Return chicken to skillet and heat. Serve immediately. Serves 4

# Parmesan Chicken

| | |
|---|---|
| 1 | cup mayonnaise-type salad dressing |
| ½ | cup Parmesan cheese |
| 2 | teaspoons oregano |
| 2-3 | pounds chicken pieces |

Mix mayonnaise-type salad dressing, Parmesan cheese and oregano. Spoon over chicken. Bake 45 minutes at 375 degrees. Serves 4-6

# Dilled Chicken Delight

| | |
|---|---|
| 2 | boneless, skinless chicken breasts |
| ¼ | cup sour cream |
| 1 | tablespoon dill dip seasoning |
| 1 | package toasted sliced almonds, if desired |
| 4 | puff pastry cups, cooked and cooled |

Cook chicken until tender. When cool, put through meat chopper and process until chicken is very fine. Mix chicken with other ingredients and blend well. Place mixture in cooked puff pastry cup. Serves 4

# Marinated Chicken Teriyaki

| | |
|---|---|
| 2 | chickens cut into ⅛'s, with or without skin |
| ¼ | cup soy sauce |
| ½ | teaspoon grated fresh ginger |
| ¼ | cup sherry |
| ½ | teaspoon dry mustard |
| 3-4 | cloves garlic, crushed |
| | juice of 1 lemon |
| ¼ | cup olive oil |
| | paprika |
| | fresh dill, chopped |

Mix together soy sauce, ginger, sherry, mustard, garlic, lemon juice and olive oil. Place chicken in marinade and marinate for ½ day in refrigerator, turning occasionally. Remove from marinade and place in baking dish. Sprinkle with paprika and fresh chopped dill before baking.

Bake for 30 to 40 minutes at 375 degrees or until done. Baste with marinate during baking. Serves 12

# Whole Turkey on the Grill

10-13 pound whole turkey

Marinade

| | |
|---|---|
| 1 | pound butter or margarine |
| 1 | cup lemon juice |
| 1 | cup Worcestershire sauce |
| 1 | tablespoon salt |
| 1 | tablespoon paprika |
| 1 | tablespoon seasoned flavor enhancer |
| ½ | cup dry sherry |
| | dry white wine |

Prepare marinade: Combine all ingredients except sherry and white wine in a saucepan and bring to a slow boil. Remove from heat and add sherry.

Prepare and clean turkey. Rinse and pat dry. Lightly sprinkle cavity with salt. Refrigerate until grill is ready.

Prepare covered grill. Place a drip pan in the center of the grill and surround by coals. If desired, add hickory chips, which have been soaked in water for 30 minutes. Place clean turkey on the center of the grill over drip pan. Insert meat thermometer into thickest part of thigh. Fill the turkey cavity with dry white wine to a depth of ½ to 1 inch. Baste well with marinade. Close grill top.

Cook, basting frequently with marinade until turkey reaches an internal temperature of 175 degrees and is done (2-3 hours). Add additional coals as needed. Serves 10-16

# Southwestern Grilled Chicken Olé

| | |
|---|---|
| 5 | chicken breasts |
| ¼ | cup Italian dressing |
| 1 | cup long grain white rice |
| 2 | cups water |
| 1 | tablespoon butter |
| 2 | cups green chili sauce, divided |
| 2 | cups cooked black beans |
| 1 | cup grated Monterey Jack, cheddar cheese mixture |
| | freshly grated black pepper to taste |
| | dash cayenne pepper |

Marinate chicken breasts in Italian dressing for several hours and grill until done. Slice chicken into small strips. Set aside.

Cook rice with water and butter for 30 minutes until tender. Spread rice in bottom of baking pan. Cover with 1 cup of chili sauce. Top with black beans. Cover with remaining green chili sauce. Add sliced grilled chicken pieces.

Bake in 350 degree oven for 20 minutes. Remove from oven and sprinkle cheese on top. Return to oven for 10 minutes. Serve immediately.

# Chicken Paprikash

| | |
|---|---|
| 2 | tablespoons butter |
| 2 | medium onions, finely chopped |
| 2 | teaspoons salt |
| 2 | tablespoons Hungarian sweet paprika |
| 4 | whole chicken breasts, halved |
| 2 | cups chicken broth |
| 2 | teaspoons flour |
| 2 | cups sour cream (low fat may be substituted) |

Heat butter in skillet and sauté onions. Sprinkle with salt, and paprika. Add chicken, browning both sides. Add broth, cover and simmer 45 minutes until tender.

Remove chicken from skillet when cool enough, remove skin and bones, and lay aside.

Combine flour and sour cream into the drippings in the skillet, stirring rapidly with a wire whisk. (If sauce is lumpy, put through a sieve). Add the chicken and heat thoroughly just to the boiling point. Do not boil.

Serve immediately over rice or small white potatoes. Garnish with sprinkles of paprika for color and flavor. Serves 4

# Chicken Quiche

3   chicken breasts, cooked and chopped
1   package chopped broccoli
6   eggs well beaten
1   cup shredded Swiss cheese
½   cup chopped green onions (include bottoms)
1   cup light cream (half-and-half)
1   cup milk
2   teaspoons prepared mustard
    dash cayenne pepper
    pastry for pie shell

Beat eggs lightly. Combine cheese, cream, milk, mustard and cayenne. Pour egg mixture over chicken and broccoli. Mix until combined well. Pour into pie shell. Bake at 375 degrees for 40 minutes or until golden brown and well set.

# Chicken Cordon Bleu with Mushroom Sauce

12   chicken breasts, halved or whole
    ham slices
    Muenster cheese slices
2   eggs, beaten with 1 tablespoon water and salt
    margarine and corn oil
Mushroom Sauce
1   can ready-to-serve chicken broth
    drippings from browned chicken
3-4   tablespoons margarine
½-1   cup white wine
1   (4 ounce) can sliced mushrooms
3-4   tablespoons flour

Tenderize chicken breasts to flatten.

Put a sliced piece of ham and cheese to fit slightly smaller on breast. Roll.

Dip in beaten egg and pat with crumbs. Set aside (this can be put in the refrigerator an hour or two before cooking. You will not need tooth-picks because the egg makes it all stick together in the refrigerator).

Brown breasts in margarine and oil. Place in baking dish.

Mushroom sauce: melt butter in pan. Add drippings, then chicken stock. Cook until boiling point. Add wine and mushrooms. Mix flour with water and add to sauce. Cook a few minutes. Pour over breasts. Bake at 325 degrees for 1 hour, basting occasionally. Serves 6-12

# Seafood

# Crusted Salmon with Herbed Mayonnaise

**Herbed Mayonnaise**

| | | |
|---|---|---|
| ⅓ | cup minced fresh Italian parsley |
| ⅓ | cup minced fresh cilantro |
| ¼ | cup minced green onion |
| 2 | tablespoons red wine vinegar |
| ½ | teaspoon minced garlic |
| ¼ | teaspoon dried oregano |
| ¼ | teaspoon freshly ground black pepper |
| ⅛ | teaspoon cayenne pepper |
| 1 | cup prepared mayonnaise |

**Fish**

| | | |
|---|---|---|
| ¼ | cup chopped fresh Italian parsley |
| ¼ | cup freshly grated Parmesan cheese |
| 2 | tablespoons chopped fresh thyme or 2 teaspoons dried thyme |
| 1 | teaspoon finely grated lemon zest |
| ¼ | teaspoon salt |
| 2 | small cloves garlic, peeled |
| 1¼ | cups fresh white bread crumbs |
| ¼ | cup butter (½ stick), melted, divided |
| 2½ | pounds salmon fillet, 1 piece if available |

Herbed Mayonnaise: In small bowl, combine minced parsley, cilantro, green onions, vinegar, garlic, oregano, pepper, and cayenne. Stir until well blended and let stand 30 minutes at room temperature, or cover with plastic wrap and chill overnight.

In food processor or blender, combine chopped parsley, Parmesan, thyme, lemon zest, and salt. With processor running, drop garlic through feed tube and process until finely chopped. Transfer to large bowl and add breadcrumbs. Toss to blend. (May be prepared in advance.) Add 3 tablespoons of the melted butter and toss.

Pat salmon dry and place, skin side down, in greased large, shallow baking pan. Brush with remaining 1 tablespoon melted butter. Pack crumb mixture on salmon. Bake 20-25 minutes in preheated oven at 450 degrees or until center is opaque. If using several small fillets, cook for 10 minutes per inch of thickness. If crumbs brown too quickly, cover loosely with foil.

Transfer to serving platter. Stir mayonnaise into chilled herb mixture and serve on the side. Serves 6

# Baked Salmon with Creole Mustard Sauce

Sauce

| | | |
|---|---|---|
| 1 | cup whipping cream |
| ¼ | cup Creole mustard or other coarse-grained mustard |
| 4 | teaspoons Worcestershire sauce |
| 1 | tablespoon Dijon mustard |
| ¼ | teaspoon ground black pepper |
| ½ | teaspoon dried basil |
| ½ | teaspoon ground white pepper |
| ¼ | teaspoon cayenne pepper |
| 1 | cup sour cream (Add just before serving to other sauce ingredients.) |

Fish

| | | |
|---|---|---|
| 2 | (1½ pound) center-cut salmon fillets |
| ¼ | cup (½ stick) unsalted butter |
| 3 | tablespoons golden brown sugar |
| 3 | tablespoons soy sauce |
| 2 | tablespoons fresh lemon juice |
| 2 | tablespoons dry white wine |

Sauce: Combine cream, Creole mustard, Worcestershire sauce, Dijon mustard, black pepper, basil, white pepper, and cayenne pepper. Simmer until very thick, stirring frequently, about 5 minutes (Can be prepared 1 day ahead. Cover and refrigerate.)

Fish: Line large baking pan with foil. Arrange fish skin side down in single layer on foil. Mix butter, brown sugar, soy sauce, lemon juice, and dry white wine in bowl. Pour over fish. Cover and refrigerate at least 1 hour and up to 6 hours. Preheat oven to 400 degrees. Uncover fish and bake until just cooked through, about 18 minutes. Baste occasionally with pan drippings. Meanwhile, rewarm sauce over low heat, stirring constantly. Add sour cream and whisk just until heated through; do not boil. Season sauce to taste with salt.

Arrange salmon on platter. Serve, passing sauce separately. Serves 6

# Salmon in Scotch Whiskey

¾  pound salmon fillets
1  ounce single malt whiskey
2  tablespoons grated lemon rind
2  tablespoons sugar

Topping

2  tablespoons minced fresh ginger
1  tablespoon sugar
1  small onion, chopped
   juice from ½ lemon
1  tablespoon butter

Marinate salmon in whiskey, sugar, and lemon rind mixture for several hours, skin side up.

Grill fish with skin side down first, then turn.

Meanwhile, prepare topping as follows: Sauté onion, sugar, and ginger. When sugar begins to caramelize, add juice of lemon. Finish with butter. Serve over grilled fish. Serves 2

*One of our editors and her husband had this in a restaurant overlooking the city of Vancouver, B.C.*

# Scallops and Green Peppers

1    pound scallops
1½   tablespoons cornstarch
2    tablespoons sherry
1    tablespoon soy sauce
2    green peppers, chopped
3    scallions, chopped
¼    pound mushrooms, sliced
3    tablespoons peanut oil
1    chicken bouillon cube
½    cup boiling water

Rinse, then slice the scallops and put in a bowl. Combine the cornstarch, sherry and soy sauce, and mix with the scallops. (This can be done anytime during the day and refrigerated, if desired.) In large frying pan, sauté peppers, mushrooms, and scallions for 2-5 minutes. Add scallops and stir 2 minutes more. Dissolve bouillon cube in boiling water and add to scallop mixture. Cover and simmer together for 2 minutes.

*Excellent with rice or noodles.*

162

# Snapper Meunière

| | |
|---|---|
| 4 | (6 to 8 ounce) snapper fillets |
| 4 | tablespoons butter |
| ¾ | cup white wine |
| 2 | tablespoons chopped capers |
| ½ | cup whipping cream |
| | juice from 2 lemons |
| | dash hot pepper sauce |
| 2 | tablespoons fresh parsley, chopped |
| | salt |

Dip fillets in flour. Melt butter in large skillet. Sauté fillets until golden brown on both sides using medium to low heat . Add wine, capers, cream, lemon juice, and hot pepper sauce. Sprinkle with parsley. Simmer until liquid thickens enough to make a sauce. Salt to taste. Serves 4

*Any white fish fillet can be used.*

# Louisiana Gumbo

| | |
|---|---|
| 1 | cup oil |
| 2 | cups all-purpose flour |
| 1 | cup chopped green onions |
| 1 | cup finely chopped fresh parsley |
| 1 | gallon fish stock, chicken stock or water |
| 1 | tablespoon poultry seasoning |
| 2 | tablespoons minced garlic |
| | salt to taste |
| | ground cayenne pepper to taste |
| 1 | pound shrimp, cleaned and peeled |
| 1 | pound chicken breast cubed |
| 1 | pound link sausage cubed |
| 6 | crab bodies, broken in half |
| | other seafood you may like |

In a large skillet, brown chicken breast and link sausage and set aside. Heat the oil in a large, heavy pot over medium heat, then stir in the flour and make a dark roux: this should take about 45 minutes.

To the roux add the onions and parsley, stirring after each addition. Cook, stirring frequently, until vegetables are tender.

Slowly add 1 cup of the stock, stirring until it forms a thick paste. Stir in the poultry seasoning, garlic and remaining stock, then add salt and pepper and stir. Bring to a boil. Add the shrimp, chicken, sausage, and crabs. Reduce the heat to low and simmer, covered, for a least 2 hours, stirring occasionally. Serve over cooked rice. Yields 6 to 10 servings

163

# Tuna with Mango Avocado Salsa

Mango Avocado Salsa

| | | |
|---|---|---|
| 2 | fresh mangos, peeled, seeded and chopped |
| ⅔ | cup diced red bell pepper |
| 2 | tablespoons chopped fresh cilantro |
| ⅓ | cup minced red onion |
| 2 | tablespoons white wine vinegar |
| 1 | tablespoon sugar |
| ½ | teaspoon salt |
| 1 | teaspoon freshly ground pepper |
| 1 | tablespoon olive oil |
| 1 | avocado |

Tuna

| | |
|---|---|
| 6 | (6 ounce) tuna or sword-fish steaks |
| | salt and fresh ground pepper |
| 2 | tablespoons white wine vinegar |
| 1 | tablespoon sugar |
| 1 | tablespoon olive oil |

In a glass bowl, combine mangos, bell pepper, cilantro, red onion, vinegar, sugar, salt, pepper, and olive oil. Chill 30 minutes.

Season tuna with salt and pepper to taste. Combine vinegar, sugar, and olive oil. Drizzle over tuna. Let stand at room temperature for 30 minutes. Preheat grill to medium. Grill tuna 10 minutes per inch of thickness, turning once.

Just before serving, peel, seed, and dice avocado and add to salsa mixture. Stir to blend and adjust seasoning to taste. Serve salsa over tuna. Serves 6

# Barbecued Jumbo Shrimp

| | |
|---|---|
| 2 | pounds jumbo shrimp (20-24 count) |
| 3 | cloves garlic, minced |
| 1 | medium onion, minced |
| ¼ | cup minced parsley |
| 1 | dried basil |
| 1 | teaspoon prepared mustard |
| 1 | teaspoon salt |
| ½ | cup olive oil |
| 1 | lemon, juiced |

Split shrimp shells up the back. Remove veins, but leave shells on. Marinate 1 hour in mixture of garlic, onion, parsley, basil, mustard, salt, oil, and lemon juice. Thread shrimp onto skewers. Broil over hot coals for about 3 minutes on each side, until shrimp turn opaque. Serves 4-6

*Do not marinate in a metal pan.*
*Terrific as an appetizer or entrée.*

164

# Shrimp Jambalaya

| | |
|---|---|
| ½ | cup sliced scallions |
| ½ | cup chopped Spanish onions |
| 2 | teaspoons olive oil |
| 4 | cloves garlic, minced |
| 1 | cup whole tomatoes, chopped |
| 1½ | cups low sodium chicken broth |
| 2 | teaspoons Cajun seasoning |
| ½ | teaspoon thyme leaves |
| 4 | ounces uncooked instant rice |
| 10 | ounces shrimp |

Sauté scallions and onions until brown. Add garlic and cook one minute. Lower heat, add tomatoes, broth, Cajun seasoning and thyme. Simmer 5 minutes, add rice and cover.

Stir in shrimp and cook 7 minutes. Serves 2

# Seafood Kabobs

| | |
|---|---|
| 1 | pound shrimp |
| 1 | pound sea scallops |
| 1 | (4-6 ounce) jar of jumbo stuffed green olives |
| 2-3 | large lemons cut into wedges |

Marinade

| | |
|---|---|
| ¼ | cup soy sauce |
| ¼ | cup salad oil |
| ¼ | cup lemon juice |
| ¼ | cup fresh parsley |
| ¼ | teaspoon salt, or to taste |
| ¼ | teaspoon black pepper, or to taste |

Peel and devein shrimp. Marinate overnight (or several hours) with scallops.

Alternate placing on the skewer with olives and lemon wedges. Grill until done (No more than 10 minutes. They cook rapidly.) Serves 4.

165

# Crab-Filled Jumbo Shrimp

1   (6 ounce) package long
    grain/wild rice
8   jumbo mushrooms
    (one pound)
2   green onions, minced
    (¼ cup)
1   tablespoon flour
4   tablespoons butter,
    divided
1   teaspoon black pepper
¾   cup milk
2   cups white bread cubes
    (4 slices)
1   tablespoon sherry
1   (6 ounce) package frozen
    crab, thawed, drained,
    and flaked
½   cup shredded cheddar
    cheese
8   slices of mozzarella
    cheese
1   tablespoon minced
    parsley

Prepare rice according to directions and keep warm. Remove stems from mushrooms, dice and reserve. Over medium heat, melt butter, add mushroom caps and cook 5 minutes, turning once. Remove caps to 8x8-inch cooking dish. In same skillet melt 2 more tablespoons butter and add green onions and diced mushroom stems and cook until tender. Stir in flour and pepper until blended. Gradually stir in milk and cook until slightly thickened and smooth. Stir in bread cubes, sherry, crab and cheddar cheese. Remove pan from heat.

Preheat oven to 425 degrees. Spoon crab filling into mushroom caps, mounding high.

Bake 10 minutes or until hot. Top each mushroom with a slice of mozzarella cheese and bake 3 minutes or until melted. To serve, spoon rice mixture on warm platter, arrange mushrooms on rice, sprinkle with parsley. Serves 4

# Shrimp Étouffée

¼ cup olive oil
2 tablespoons butter
1 medium onion, chopped
1 bell pepper, chopped
3 large stalks of celery, chopped
¼ teaspoon salt, or to taste
⅛ teaspoon cayenne pepper, or to taste
1 pound shrimp, peeled and deveined
2 cloves garlic, chopped
1 tablespoon Cajun spice
1 cup chopped fresh parsley
1 tablespoon flour
1 cup water
2 scallions, chopped including green parts
fresh parsley

Sauté onions, pepper, and celery in olive oil and butter for 10-15 minutes in a large frying pan. Add salt, cayenne pepper, shrimp, garlic and Cajun spice. Continue simmering for 5-10 minutes. Dissolve flour in water and add to shrimp. Cook until thickened. Taste for seasonings. Place in serving bowl and top with parsley and scallions.

*Serve with rice, crusty bread, and a tossed salad. May be prepared ahead to the point where the shrimp is added. After shrimp is added, it should be heated and served immediately.*

*This can be made with more vegetables or more shrimp (chicken or crawfish could also be used). Also, the types of peppers used can be varied, though use caution if substituting hot peppers. Red, yellow, purple or orange peppers all add visual interest to the dish. One or two hot peppers can be used in place of the cayenne pepper. Serves 4*

## Shrimp Victoria

| | |
|---|---|
| 1 | pound medium shrimp, peeled and deveined |
| ¼ | cup minced onion |
| 5 | tablespoons butter, divided |
| ½ | pound mushrooms, quartered |
| 1 | tablespoon all purpose flour |
| ¼ | teaspoon salt |
| ⅛ | teaspoon pepper |
| 1 | cup sour cream |
| 1 | red bell pepper cut into strips |
| 1 | yellow bell pepper cut into strips |

In skillet, sauté shrimp and onion in 4 tablespoons butter until shrimp are pink. Add mushrooms and cook 5 minutes more. Stir in remaining butter, flour, salt and pepper and cook for 1 minute. Slowly stir in sour cream, blending until hot and smooth. Arrange red and yellow pepper strips around shrimp. Serves 4-6

*This is a terrific luncheon entrée and is beautiful when presented in a chafing dish for a buffet. Serve with a simple lemon rice, made by adding lemon peel and lemon juice to rice while cooking.*

## Chili Shrimp

| | |
|---|---|
| 1 | pound (31-35) large shrimp |
| 1 | tablespoon salad oil |
| 1 | tablespoon minced fresh ginger |
| 3 | cloves garlic, minced or pressed |
| 3 | tablespoons catsup |
| 1 | tablespoon cider vinegar |
| 1 | tablespoon soy sauce |
| 1 | tablespoon sugar |
| ½-1 | teaspoon crushed red pepper |
| ½ | teaspoon oriental sesame oil |
| 3 | cups hot cooked rice |
| 1 | bunch sliced green onions to garnish |

Peel shrimp, leaving last section of shell on tail. Devein and rinse. Place a wok or 10-12 inch frying pan over high heat. Add salad oil. When hot, add shrimp. Stir-fry until shrimp are pink and opaque in center, about 3 minutes. With a slotted spoon, lift out shrimp, drain briefly, and set aside. To pan, add ginger and garlic. Stir-fry until garlic is tinged with gold, about 30 seconds. Add catsup, vinegar, soy sauce, sugar and chilies to taste. Stir until boiling. Add shrimp, any accumulated juices, and sesame oil. Mix well.

Mound rice on a platter. Top with shrimp mixture and garnish with sliced green onions. Serves 4

# Seafood Gumbo

1 pound headless medium shrimp in shells (may be frozen if preferred)
1 tablespoon vegetable oil
1 medium white onion, finely chopped
1-2 garlic cloves, minced
2-3 stalks celery, chopped
½-¾ pound okra, sliced
12 ounces of canned tomato juice
¼ teaspoon salt
⅛ teaspoon cayenne pepper
¼ pound fresh lump crab meat, (or 1 can crab meat)
1 cup rice prepared according to directions on box

Cook shrimp in seasoned water until they turn pink. Remove from heat and let stand 5 minutes. Drain, reserving about 2 cups shrimp stock. When shrimp are cool peel and devein. Place shrimp in refrigerator. Sauté onions and garlic in oil until tender. Set aside. In a 3-quart pan, steam celery and okra in a little water. Pour tomato juice into a 10-12 quart stockpot and add salt, pepper, and vegetables. Stir to mix well. Cover. Place on low heat and cook for 2 hours, stirring frequently. Add shrimp and cleaned crab and cook for another 30 minutes. If extra liquid is needed, use reserved shrimp stock (about 1 cup should suffice.) Serve steaming gumbo in bowls over cooked rice. Serves 4

*An excellent gumbo that does not require making a roux.*

# Orange Roughy Parmesan

2 pounds orange roughy
2 tablespoons fresh lemon juice
½ cup freshly shredded Parmesan cheese
4 tablespoons butter, softened
3 tablespoons mayonnaise
3 tablespoons chopped green onions
¼ teaspoon salt
dash red hot pepper sauce
freshly ground black pepper to taste

In a greased 9x13-inch baking dish, place fillets in a single layer. Brush with lemon juice and let stand for 10 minutes. In a small bowl, combine cheese, butter, mayonnaise, green onions, salt, pepper and red hot pepper sauce. Broil fillets 3-4 inches under preheated broiler for 5 minutes. Spread with cheese mixture and broil for an additional 2-3 minutes. Watch closely! Serves 6

*Sole or any other fresh, skinless, white fish can be substituted for orange roughy.*

# Tuna with Mango Avocado Salsa

Mango Avocado Salsa

 2 fresh mangoes, peeled, seeded and chopped
 ⅔ cup diced red bell pepper
 2 tablespoons chopped fresh cilantro
 ⅓ cup minced red onion
 2 tablespoons white wine vinegar
 1 tablespoon sugar
 ½ teaspoon salt
 1 teaspoon freshly ground pepper
 1 tablespoon olive oil
 1 avocado

Tuna

 6 (6 ounce) tuna or swordfish steaks
  salt to taste
  ground black pepper to taste
 2 tablespoons white wine vinegar
 1 tablespoon sugar
 1 tablespoon olive oil

In glass bowl, combine mangoes, bell pepper, cilantro, red onion, vinegar, sugar, salt, pepper and olive oil. Chill 30 minutes. Season tuna with salt and pepper to taste. Combine vinegar, sugar, and olive oil. Drizzle over tuna. Let stand, at room temperature 30 minutes.

Preheat grill to medium. Grill tuna 10 minutes per inch of thickness, turning once. Peel, seed and dice avocado and add to salsa mixture. Stir to blend and adjust seasoning to taste. Serve over tuna. Serves 6

*Any white fish can be used in this recipe.*

# Grilled Swordfish with Cilantro Butter

8   center cut fillets fresh swordfish (8 ounces each)
2   tablespoons olive oil
2   bunches cilantro
2   lemons, juiced
1   cup unsalted butter
   salt and pepper to taste
   oil for the grill

Prepare fire for direct-heat method of cooking. (Swordfish is especially good cooked over mesquite charcoal, although other types of fuel are fine.) Wash fish and pat dry. Lightly coat fillets with olive oil. When fire is ready, place fish on oiled grill and cook until done to the touch (about 4 minutes per side for thick fillets, less for thinner fillets.) Serve immediately with cilantro butter.

Cilantro Butter: Wash cilantro thoroughly and remove thick stems. Combine with butter in food processor or blender and mix for several seconds with metal blade until light and fluffy. Blend in lemon juice. Add salt and pepper to taste. Serves 8

# Smoked Salmon

   Salmon fillets
2   sticks of cinnamon
1   tablespoon whole cloves
½   cup sugar
1   teaspoon nutmeg
¼   teaspoon salt
2   cups water

Condiments
1   bunch dill, minced
1   (8 ounce) carton sour cream
1   small purple onion, finely minced
1   small jar capers, drained
1   package of toast rounds or melba toast

Place salmon fillets, that you have carefully searched for bones with needle-nose pliers, into a large zip-top freezer bag. Add cinnamon, cloves, sugar, nutmeg, salt, and water. Cure for 2 days in refrigerator. Smoke in smoker for 20 minutes, or until firm to the touch. Serve with dill, sour cream, chopped purple onions, capers, on toast rounds or melba toast.

# Belize "BBQ'd" Fish

2    large white-fish type fillets (like cod or orange roughy)
4    large carrots
1    sweet onion
1    red bell pepper
1    green bell pepper
2    jalapeños (optional)
2    banana peppers (optional)
1    lemon
      Greek seasoning
      garlic powder

Grate carrots and set aside. Dice onions into ¼-inch cubes and set aside. Dice bell pepper into ¼-inch cubes. If using jalapeño and/or banana peppers, slice thinly. Mix all peppers (bell and others) and set aside.

Tear off a large (12 inch) piece of aluminum foil. Spread ¼ of the grated carrots out on foil and sprinkle ¼ of the onion on top of the carrots. Sprinkle one side of the fillet with seasonings and place seasoning side down. Sprinkle seasonings on top of fillet. Cover fillet with ½ of pepper mixture, ¼ onions and ¼ carrots. Squeeze ¼ lemon over all. Fold foil so it covers fish and veggies well and seal. Repeat for other fillet.

Place on grill at medium temperature 10 minutes on each side. Serve with pepper side up. Serves 2

# Island Grilled Halibut

6    halibut steaks, 1 inch thick
2    cloves garlic
¼    teaspoon ground white pepper
2    tablespoons sugar
⅓    cup soy sauce
6    tablespoons corn oil
3    green onions, chopped
1    tablespoon sesame seeds

Combine garlic, white pepper, sugar, soy sauce, corn oil, green onions, and sesame seeds. Pour over halibut steaks. Cover and marinate in refrigerator overnight. Place steaks on grill and cook 7 minutes per side or until fish flakes easily. Serves 6

# Grilled Marinated Swordfish

Marinade

| | |
|---|---|
| 8 | small swordfish steaks |
| ½ | cup vegetable oil |
| ⅓ | cup soy sauce |
| ¼ | cup fresh lemon juice |
| 1 | teaspoon grated lemon peel |
| 1 | clove of garlic, crushed |

Avocado Butter

| | |
|---|---|
| 1 | stick butter, room temperature |
| ½ | cup mashed avocado |
| 5 | tablespoons fresh lemon juice |
| 2 | tablespoons minced parsley |
| 2 | cloves garlic, minced |
| 1 | lime, sliced |
| 1 | bunch parsley, for garnish |

Pierce fish on both sides with fork. Arrange in shallow dish. Combine oil, soy sauce, lemon juice, lemon peel, and crushed garlic. Pour this marinade over the swordfish. Cover and refrigerate for 2 hours.

Avocado Butter: Beat butter in a small bowl until soft and creamy. Add avocado, lemon juice, parsley and garlic. Cover and refrigerate until time to serve. Prepare grill. Drain marinade and save. Grill fish about 9 minutes on each side for each inch in thickness. Turn once. Serve with avocado butter on top and garnish with parsley. Serves 8

# Brenda's Grilled Salmon

1   can of vegetable spray
1   pound salmon fillet or
    mild white fish (orange
    roughy, scrod, or cod)
2   tablespoons white wine
2   tablespoons white
    Worcestershire sauce
2   tablespoons lemon juice
2   teaspoons low-fat marga-
    rine, melted

Spray wire fish basket or clean grill rack with vegetable spray. Never spray near source of heat! Preheat grill. Rinse fish and pat dry. Place in fish basket. In a small bowl combine wine, Worcestershire sauce, lemon juice and margarine. Place fish on hot grill, basting frequently with marinade. Cook about 5 minutes on high heat or until fish flakes when tested with a fork. Serves 2

*Substitutes for cooking method: Aluminum foil method: If you do not have a fish basket, lay a piece of aluminum foil over grill rack. Using a fork, pierce the foil several times. Place fish directly on foil and proceed as above. Oven Broiled: Simply spray broiler pan, place in broiler and proceed as above.*
*The husband of one of our members loves fried fish, so when they changed to a healthier style of eating, she had to be more creative in her cooking. She has created many fish recipes, but this is her husband's favorite.*

174

Pasta
and
Rice

# John Wayne's Chili Cheese Casserole

2    (4 ounce) cans chopped
     green chilies, drained
1    pound Monterey Jack
     cheese, grated
1    pound cheddar grated
4    eggs, separated
⅔    cup evaporated milk
2    tablespoons flour
½    teaspoon salt
¼    teaspoon pepper
2    tomatoes, thinly sliced
     (optional)

Place chilies and cheeses in 11x13-inch casserole dish. Beat egg whites until stiff. Separately beat the yolks with milk, flour and seasonings. Fold yolk mixture with egg whites. Marble in cheese and chilies. The top can be covered with 2 thinly sliced tomatoes.

Cook uncovered approximately 1 hour at 325 degrees. Serves 6-8

# Wild Rice with Mushrooms and Almonds

1    cup uncooked wild rice
¼    cup butter or margarine
½    cup slivered almonds
2    tablespoons snipped
     chives or chopped
     green onions
1    (8 ounce) can mushroom
     stems and pieces,
     drained
3    cups chicken broth

Soak wild rice for several hours or overnight in water. Drain.

Melt butter in large skillet. Add rice, almonds, chives and mushrooms. Cook and stir until almonds are golden brown, about 20 minutes.

Heat oven to 325 degrees. Pour rice mixture into ungreased 1½ quart casserole. Heat chicken broth to boiling; stir into rice mixture. Cover tightly.

Bake about 1½ hours or until all liquid is absorbed and rice is tender and fluffy.

Chicken broth can be made by dissolving 3 chicken bouillon cubes in 3 cups boiling water, or use canned chicken broth. Serves 6-8

# Faux Gourmet Macaroni and Cheese Casserole

1 (7 ounce) package elbow macaroni
2 cups small curd cottage cheese
1 cup sour cream
1 egg slightly beaten
¾ teaspoon salt
   dash of pepper
10 ounces sharp grated cheese or 12 ounces mild grated cheese

Cook macaroni according to package directions and drain.

Combine cottage cheese, sour cream, egg, grated cheese, salt and pepper in a large bowl.

Stir the macaroni into the above ingredients.

Pour mixture into a greased 9x9x2-inch glass baking dish. Cook 45 minutes at 350 degrees. Serves 6-8

# Summer Spaghetti

¼ cup olive oil
1 clove garlic, minced
1 green pepper, cut into julienne strips
1 onion, chopped
1 small zucchini, peeled and sliced thin
2 tomatoes, chopped
1½ teaspoons water
1 teaspoon salt
½ teaspoon dried ground red pepper
1 (6 ounce) package long, thin spaghetti, cooked according to package directions

Heat oil in skillet. Sauté onion, garlic, zucchini and green pepper for 15 minutes. Stir occasionally. Add tomatoes, water, salt and dried red pepper.

Cook over low heat for 15 minutes. Add spaghetti, mixing lightly.

*You can substitute other pasta, such as colored rotini. Also, substitute broccoli for zucchini.*

# Black Beans and Rice - St. Louis Style

| | |
|---|---|
| 2 | cups black beans |
| 3 | quarts water |
| ½ | pound ham, cubed |
| 2 | tablespoons olive oil |
| 2 | medium onions, chopped |
| 2 | cloves garlic, minced |
| ½ | cup celery, chopped |
| 1 | green pepper, chopped |
| 1 | tablespoon paprika |
| 2 | tablespoons butter |
| 2 | tablespoons flour |
| 3 | tablespoons rum |
| 3 | carrots, chopped |
| | salt and pepper to taste |

Soak beans overnight. Drain. Combine beans, 3 quarts of water, salt, paprika, ham; cover and cook on low for 3 hours.

Heat oil in large skillet; add onions, garlic, carrots, celery and green pepper. Sauté for 15 minutes. Add to beans, cover and cook.

Knead butter and flour together, forming a ball. Add to soup, stir frequently and bring to a boil. Add rum. Stir until ball melts, then cover and cook for 1-3 hours, it is up to you.

Just before serving, mash a few beans against the side of the pot to thicken soup and cook for another ten minutes. Have plenty of finely chopped sweet onions, grated cheese, and hot pepper sauce to top off. Serve with white rice. Serves 8-10

# Nancy's Wild Rice

| | |
|---|---|
| 1 | (6-8 ounce) package long grain and wild rice mix water and sherry |
| 2-3 | chopped green onions |
| ½ | teaspoon garlic powder |
| 4-5 | large mushrooms, sliced and slightly sautéed in 1 tablespoon butter |
| 1 | tablespoon fresh or dried rosemary, crushed |
| 1 | (8 ounce) can chopped water chestnuts |

Prepare rice according to directions, substituting sherry for half the water called for. Cook until fairly dry. When done, stir in remaining ingredients and turn into a greased baking dish. Bake at 350 degrees for about 30 minutes. Serves 6

*May add cooked chicken or pork for a one-dish meal.*

178

# Risotto with Shrimp

**Shrimp broth**

1   pound medium shrimp, cleaned, deveined, reserving shells
1   clove garlic, chopped
1   medium onion, chopped
¼-⅓   cup chopped carrot
1   stalk celery, chopped
1   tablespoon parsley
2   tablespoons olive oil
    salt and pepper to taste
5   cups water

**Risotto**

¼   cup chopped onion
1   clove garlic, chopped
1   tablespoon unsalted butter
2   tablespoons olive oil
1   cup Arborio rice
½   cup dry wine
1   small tomato diced
¼   cup grated Parmesan cheese, optional

Place shrimp shells in large saucepan. Add onion, carrot, celery, parsley, water and salt to taste. Simmer gently 20-25 minutes. Strain, discard shells and vegetables, reserve broth and set aside.

Heat 2 tablespoons oil in large skillet, and sauté garlic lightly. Add shrimp, salt and freshly ground pepper to taste and sauté just until pink. Set aside. Shrimp may be cut in half, if desired.

In large pot or skillet, over medium heat, combine oil and butter. Sauté onion and garlic until wilted but not brown.

Add rice, stir to coat. Add a cup of the reserved shrimp broth and cook, stirring frequently until rice has absorbed liquid. Add diced tomato and wine. Continue cooking and stirring, adding broth 1 cup at a time, until rice is creamy and tender but al dente (about 3 cups). This should take about 18 minutes.

Add shrimp during last 5 minutes of cooking. Add more broth if necessary. Stir in cheese just before serving. One tablespoon of butter can also be mixed in at the end for extra creaminess. Serve immediately.
Serves 4

179

# Pasta with Asparagus

1 pound pasta such as ziti or rigatoni

⅓ cup oil (olive preferably, or canola)

2-3 garlic cloves

1 cup peeled plum tomatoes, fresh or canned, cut into pieces

½ teaspoon salt

1 pound fresh asparagus

2 eggs

4-6 tablespoons freshly grated Romano or Parmesan cheese

 freshly ground pepper to taste

Sauté garlic cloves in oil in large, uncovered frying pan until golden and then discard cloves. Add tomatoes to the flavored oil, mashing them in. Add salt and cook for about 15 minutes, stirring occasionally, until the tomatoes have darkened and reduced.

Meanwhile, break off and discard the tough bottoms from the asparagus and cut the remainder into bite size pieces. Cook in a large pot of boiling, salted water until tender but slightly crisp. Drain completely and cool.

Beat the eggs in the pasta serving bowl. Add the cooked asparagus, lots of ground pepper, and the grated cheese. Cook and drain the pasta and immediately add to the asparagus and eggs. Toss gently, letting the heat of the pasta cook the eggs. Add the tomato sauce, toss again, and serve immediately. Serves 6

*This is similar to Pasta Carbonara, but uses asparagus instead of bacon - good for vegetarians.*

180

*Photo on right ~*
Mexican Chicken Mole, page 146

# Shrimp Fettuccini

| | |
|---|---|
| 3 | sticks butter |
| 3 | medium onions, chopped |
| 3 | stalks celery, chopped |
| 2 | green peppers, chopped |
| ¼ | cup flour |
| 4 | tablespoons fresh parsley, chopped |
| 3 | pounds shrimp, shelled, deveined |
| 1 | pint half-and-half |
| 1 | pound processed cheese loaf, cubed |
| 2 | tablespoons jalapeños, chopped |
| 3 | garlic cloves, crushed |
| | salt and pepper to taste |
| 1 | pound fettuccini noodles, cooked according to directions |
| | Parmesan cheese, for garnish |

Melt butter in heavy saucepan, medium heat. Add onion, celery, and bell pepper. Cook 10 minutes or until onion is clear. Add parsley and shrimp, cook 10 minutes, stirring often. Add flour, blend well. Cover and cook 10-15 minutes. Stir often if not in non-stick pot.

Add half-and-half, cheese, jalapeño and garlic. Stir well. Add salt and pepper to taste.

Cook covered over low heat 20 minutes, stirring occasionally. Add shrimp mixture to hot cooked fettuccini. Mix thoroughly. May be frozen at this point, will keep up to 3 months.

Pour into buttered 3 quart casserole (or 2 large dishes). Sprinkle with Parmesan cheese. Bake at 350 degrees for 15-20 minutes. Serves 10-12

*Photo on left ~*
Barbeque by the Cement
Pond, page 16

181

# Linguini with White Clam Sauce

1    clove garlic, minced
4    tablespoons butter
2    tablespoons all-purpose
     flour
2    cups bottled clam juice
¼    cup minced fresh parsley
     or 1 tablespoon dried
     parsley
1½   teaspoons dried thyme
¼    teaspoon salt
¼    teaspoon freshly ground
     black pepper
2    cups fresh clams, minced
     or 3 (6¼-ounce) cans
     minced clams
12   ounces linguini, cooked al
     dente and drained

In large skillet, sauté garlic in butter over medium-high heat for 1 minute. Whisk in flour until smooth and add clam juice. Whisk until mixed.

Add parsley, thyme, salt and pepper. Reduce heat and simmer for 10 minutes or until sauce is reduced by ⅓. Add clams and heat through.

Place warm linguini in heated serving dish. Pour sauce over linguini and toss gently. Serve immediately. Serves 4-6 main dish or 8-10 side dish

*The secret of this sauce is reducing the clam juice so the flavor is intensified.*

# Ranch Style Fettuccini

½    cup butter
2    zucchini, julienne sliced
1    carrot, julienne sliced
8    ounces fresh mushrooms,
     sliced
¼    pound green onions,
     sliced
½    teaspoon basil
1½   cups chopped cooked ham
½    teaspoon salt
⅛    teaspoon pepper
1    cup frozen green peas,
     thawed
8    ounces cooked fettuccini
½    cup grated Parmesan
     cheese

Melt butter in skillet over medium heat. Add zucchini and carrot; sauté until tender.

Stir in mushrooms, green onions, basil, salt and pepper, cook 2 minutes.

Add peas and ham, cook until hot.

Cook fettuccini, drain. Add cheese, ham and vegetables to fettuccini and toss lightly. Serves 5-6

# Pasta Primavera Alfredo

## Pasta Primavera

| | |
|---|---|
| 1 | pound spaghetti |
| 1 | zucchini, sliced ¼ inch thick |
| ½ | pound broccoli, cut into 1 inch flowerettes |
| 1 | sweet red bell pepper, cut into strips (a must even if just for appearance) |
| ½ | pound whole fresh snow peas or fresh green beans (snip ends off) |
| 1 | tablespoon margarine |
| 2 | tablespoons oil |

Cook spaghetti according to directions (until al dente). Meanwhile, sauté vegetables in butter and oil until crisp and tender, but not limp. Season to taste with salt, pepper and sugar. While vegetables are cooking make alfredo sauce.

## Alfredo Sauce

| | |
|---|---|
| 1 | clove garlic, minced |
| 1 | cup whipping cream |
| ¼ | cup butter (half stick), do not use margarine |
| ½ | cup freshly grated Parmesan cheese |
| ¼ | teaspoon salt |
| | coarse black pepper |

Sauté garlic in butter. Add unwhipped cream and Parmesan cheese. Simmer over low heat for 10 minutes. Season to taste with salt and pepper. Pour over vegetables. Drain cooked spaghetti.

Top with alfredo sauce and vegetables. Serve hot with extra Parmesan cheese sprinkled on top. Serves 4

183

# West 38th Street Pasta Special

½ pound sweet Italian sausage, casings removed

½ pound hot Italian sausage, casings removed

½ cup olive oil

½ cup butter

12 large mushrooms, sliced

2 cloves garlic, minced

1 large green bell pepper, seeded and chopped

1 cup chopped green onions

¼ cup minced fresh parsley

¼ cup minced fresh basil or 2 teaspoons dried basil

12 ounces spinach fettuccini, cooked al dente and drained

⅔ cup freshly grated Parmesan cheese

1 cup sour cream

In large skillet, cook sausages over medium-high heat until brown. Remove sausage and set aside. Drain grease.

Add olive oil and butter to skillet and sauté mushrooms, garlic, green pepper, green onions, parsley and basil until tender. Place fettuccini in heated serving dish. Add sausage mixture, Parmesan and sour cream. Toss gently and serve immediately. Serves 6

# Spaghetti with Fried Eggplant

| | |
|---|---|
| 1 | medium eggplant |
| | vegetable oil (canola, corn) for frying |
| 2 | garlic cloves |
| 3 | tablespoons olive oil |
| 2 | cups peeled tomatoes, fresh or canned, cut in chunks |
| 10 | fresh basil leaves, chopped coarsely |
| 1 | teaspoon salt |
| | freshly ground pepper |
| 4 | ounces crumbled feta cheese |
| ½ | pound spaghetti, linguine, or vermicelli |

Slice eggplant into ¼ inch slices and then into thin strips about 2 inches long. Fry the eggplant, a few at a time in vegetable oil that has been brought to high heat, until the eggplant is golden and crisp. Remove the slices from the oil with a slotted spoon and drain on absorbent paper. Repeat until done.

Meanwhile cut garlic cloves in half and sauté in a large frying pan in olive oil until golden; discard the garlic. Add tomatoes to flavored oil after it has cooled slightly. Add the basil, salt and pepper and simmer for about 20 minutes until thickened and darker. Taste for seasonings.

Cook and drain the pasta and place into a large serving container. Dress with the tomato sauce and toss well. Spread the eggplant over the pasta and sprinkle with the crumbled cheese. Toss gently and serve immediately. Serves 2 main course or 4 first course

# Zesty Macaroni and Cheese

| | |
|---|---|
| 1 | tablespoon salad oil |
| 1 | small onion, minced |
| 2 | (16 ounce) cans tomatoes |
| 1 | (16 ounce) can tomato paste |
| 1 | teaspoon dried basil |
| 1 | teaspoon salt |
| ½ | teaspoon sugar |
| ½ | teaspoon ground oregano |
| 1 | (8 ounce) package elbow macaroni (or 8 ounces any macaroni) |
| 1 | (8 ounce) container cottage cheese |
| 1 | (8 ounce) package process cheese, cubed (about 1½ cups) |
| 2 | tablespoons butter or margarine |

In large skillet, sauté onion in hot oil until tender, about 5 minutes. Drain tomatoes; stir in tomatoes, tomato paste, basil, salt, sugar, and oregano. Simmer covered over low heat about 20 minutes, stirring occasionally.

Meanwhile, cook macaroni as directed, drain. Preheat oven to 350 degrees. Mix macaroni with tomato sauce mixture, cottage cheese, cheese cubes, and butter or margarine. Pour mixture into buttered 2½ quart casserole. Bake 30 minutes or until hot and bubbly. Serves 8

*To do ahead, mix ingredients and refrigerate. Increase baking time to 35 minutes or bake until hot and bubbly.*

Vegetables
and
Side Dishes

# Savory Green Beans with Shallots

| | | |
|---|---|---|
| 4 | slices lean bacon | |
| ½ | cup shallots or white part of green onion, minced | |
| 2 | tablespoons herb vinegar, such as tarragon | |
| 1 | teaspoon Dijon style mustard | |
| 1 | pound fresh green beans, cut French style (on the diagonal) | |
| 2 | tablespoons chives, chopped | |
| | salt and pepper to taste | |

In a skillet, fry the bacon until crisp. Drain on paper towel, then crumble into small bits.

Sauté the shallots or onion in the bacon fat until tender, but not browned.

Stir in the vinegar and mustard and set aside.

Cook the beans in boiling water for 5-6 minutes until tender. Drain well.

Add the beans to the skillet and toss well. Season with salt and pepper to taste. Sprinkle with the reserved bacon and chopped chives. Serve warm. Serves 4

# Chinese Noodles

| | |
|---|---|
| ½ | cup peanut oil |
| 2 | tablespoons rice vinegar or white wine vinegar |
| 1 | tablespoon dry sherry |
| 2½ | tablespoons sesame oil |
| 3 | tablespoons soy sauce |
| 1 | tablespoon crushed red pepper |
| ½ | teaspoon ground ginger |
| 1 | tablespoon brown sugar |
| 1 | tablespoon chopped onion |
| ¼ | cup diced green pepper |
| 1½ | pound spaghetti, cooked al dente and drained |

Combine all ingredients. Toss well and refrigerate 2 hours. Stir occasionally. Serves 8

# Hot Curried Fruit

½    cup margarine
¾    cup brown sugar
1½   teaspoon curry powder
1    (30 ounce) can sliced
     peaches
1    (30 ounce) can pear
     halves
1    (20 ounce) can chunk
     pineapple
1    (20 ounce) can apricot
     halves
1    (8 ounce) jar maraschino
     cherries
2    bananas, sliced

Melt margarine, add brown sugar and curry powder. Stir together until well mixed. Drain all fruit and put in large shallow casserole. Pour margarine mixture over fruit and bake one hour at 300 degrees. Serves 10-12

# Pineapple Bake

½    cup butter or margarine
1    cup sugar
4    eggs
¾    drained crushed pineapple
¾    cup cut-up orange sec-
     tions
5    slices day-old bread, cut
     in cubes

Cream butter and sugar in large mixing bowl. Add eggs and beat well. Add pineapple and orange sections. Stir in bread cubes. Pour mixture into greased 1½ quart casserole. Bake uncovered at 350 degrees for 50-60 minutes, or until lightly browned. Serve hot or cold. Serves 6

# Candied Carrots

1    pound carrots
1    cup orange marmalade
1    teaspoon cornstarch

Cut carrots crosswise into ¼ inch thick pieces. Drop in sauce pan containing a small amount of boiling water and boil about 5 minutes. Add marmalade, cook until tender. Thicken remaining liquid with cornstarch.

189

# Vegetable Mixed Grill with Aioli Sauce

2 medium eggplants (about 1 pound each)
2 pounds zucchini
2 pounds yellow pattypan squash
4 red bell peppers
2 bunches green onions
1 cup olive oil
4 tablespoons minced garlic
   salt and pepper to taste
2 lemons, optional

Wash all vegetables and pat dry, leaving stems on eggplant, zucchini, and pattypan squash. Cut eggplant lengthwise into 1-inch thick slices. Cut zucchini lengthwise into 1-inch thick steaks. Quarter pattypan squash. Stem and seed peppers and cut into quarters lengthwise. Remove roots from green onions. On a baking sheet mix oil, garlic and salt and pepper. Rub all surfaces of vegetables with oil mixture. Be sure surfaces of eggplant and squash are well covered.

Prepare fire for direct heat method cooking. If using a gas grill, use presoaked hardwood chips for a smoky flavor complement. If using charcoal, use presoaked hardwood chunks. When fire is ready, place all vegetables on grill. Quick hands and a pair of tongs are important because the oil covering will cause flare-ups; close the lid as soon as possible. Be sure to lay vegetables crossways to grill so they don't fall into the briquettes. After 5-6 minutes, flip vegetables over with a spatula. Moisten with extra oil if surfaces appear to be drying out rather than cooking. (Eggplant is particularly susceptible to this problem.) Close lid. Vegetables should be done in another 5-6 minutes. Add a squeeze of lemon juice on vegetables as they are cooking. Serve immediately with Aioli Sauce. Serves 8

*(continued on next page)*

Aioli Sauce

| | |
|---|---|
| 12 | cloves of garlic, minced |
| 2 | egg yolks |
| 2 | cups olive oil |
| 2 | teaspoons tepid water |
| | juice of 1 lemon |
| | salt and pepper to taste |

Aioli is a garlicky homemade mayonnaise. In a small bowl combine garlic and egg yolk. Slowly dribble olive oil in to bowl and whisk in. Mixture will begin to build up into a thick cream. Add the tepid water and part of lemon juice, as sauce becomes too thick. Continue to add olive oil, then remainder of lemon juice. Season to taste with salt and pepper. Serve at room temperature or chill if desired. Makes 2 cups

# 1015 Onion Pie

| | |
|---|---|
| 1 | unbaked pie shell |
| 1 | pound 1015 Texas sweet onions, chopped |
| 2 | tablespoons butter |
| | salt and pepper to taste |
| 2 | tablespoons flour |
| 2 | eggs |
| 1 | cup half-and-half or heavy cream |
| | pinch nutmeg |
| | pinch garlic powder |
| | dash hot pepper sauce |
| ¼ | cup grated Parmesan and/or Romano cheese |

Sauté onions in butter and remove from pan. Sprinkle onions with salt, pepper and flour. Beat eggs, add cream, other seasonings and cheeses. Mix onions with cream mixture and pour into pie shell. Bake at 375 degrees for 30-45 minutes and serve hot. Garnish with paprika and chopped parsley. Serves 6-8

*Any sweet onion may be used.*

# Steamed Asparagus with Almond Butter

8   tablespoons (1 stick) unsalted butter, room temperature
3   tablespoons finely chopped shallots
1   large garlic clove, minced
3   tablespoons chopped fresh parsley
2   teaspoons fresh lemon juice
2   teaspoons grated lemon peel
2   pounds asparagus, trimmed
½   cup sliced almonds

Melt 2 tablespoons butter in heavy small skillet over low heat. Add shallots and garlic and sauté until tender, about 5 minutes. Pour into medium bowl. Add remaining 6 tablespoons butter, parsley, lemon juice and lemon peel to shallot mixture and whisk to blend. Season to taste with salt and pepper. Steam asparagus until crisp-tender. Place butter mixture in heavy large skillet over medium heat. Add almonds and cook until butter browns, stirring occasionally, about 3 minutes. Add asparagus and stir until heated through. Season to taste with salt and pepper. Serves 8

*Can be prepared 1 day ahead to point of putting the butter mixture in a heavy skillet. Cover butter mixture and asparagus separately and chill.*

# Spinach Feta Casserole

1½  pound fresh spinach
½   cup feta cheese crumbled
½   teaspoon dill weed
    dash garlic powder
¾   cup seasoned dry bread crumb mix (as for turkey stuffing)
2   tablespoons melted margarine

Wash, cook and drain spinach. Press out as much water as possible. Chop spinach and mix with cheese, dill and garlic powder. Put in casserole. Top with dry bread crumbs. Drizzle melted margarine over crumb topping. Brown topping in very hot oven or under the broiler for 15-20 minutes. Serves 4

192

# Spinach-Artichoke Casserole

2    (10 ounce) packages
     frozen chopped spin-
     ach, thawed and well
     drained
1    (6 ounce) jar marinated
     artichoke hearts,
     drained and chopped
1    (8 ounce) package cream
     cheese, softened
2    tablespoons butter or
     margarine, softened
¼    cup milk
¼    teaspoon freshly ground
     pepper
2    tablespoons grated
     Parmesan cheese

Combine spinach and artichokes in a large bowl. Combine cream cheese and next 3 ingredients; stir into spinach mixture. Spoon mixture into a lightly greased 1½ quart casserole. Sprinkle with Parmesan cheese. Bake covered at 350 degrees for 30 minutes; uncover and bake an additional 10 minutes. Serves 6

# Guilt Free Creamed Spinach

4    dried tomato halves
½    cup boiling water
2    (10 ounce) packages
     frozen spinach, thawed
     small shallots, minced
1    clove garlic, minced
1    tablespoon cornstarch
1    cup low-fat milk
¼    cup grated Parmesan
     cheese
½    cup nonfat sour cream
½    teaspoon salt
¼    teaspoon ground pepper

In small bowl, combine tomatoes and the boiling water. Set aside. In skillet, heat spinach over medium-high heat 10 minutes or until liquid evaporates. Place in bowl. Remove tomatoes from water; finely chop. Pour water from tomatoes into same skillet; add shallots and garlic. Cover; over medium heat, cook 10 minutes or until shallots are soft and translucent. In bowl, blend corn-starch with milk. Stir into shallot mixture; heat, stirring, until boiling. Cook 1 minute. Add spinach and tomatoes; cook, stirring 1 minute. Stir in sour cream, salt and pepper, until sour cream melts (do not simmer). Serves 6

193

## Company Peas

| | |
|---|---|
| ¼ | cup butter |
| 1 | cup braised celery |
| ¼ | cup chopped onion |
| ½ | teaspoon savory or marjoram |
| ½ | teaspoon salt |
| ¼ | teaspoon pepper |
| 1 | (4 ounce) jar pimento |
| 1 | (20 ounce) package frozen peas |
| 1 | (8 ounce) can sliced water chestnuts |

Sauté celery, onion in melted butter and savory and other seasonings. Add pimento and sauté. Add cooked peas and water chestnuts. Heat thoroughly. Serves 8

*Variation: Add mushrooms.*

## Minted Peas in Boston Lettuce Cups

| | |
|---|---|
| 1 | (10 ounce) package frozen peas |
| ½ | cup unsalted butter |
| 1 | onion, medium sized halved and thinly sliced |
| ⅓ | cup minced fresh mint leaves |
| 1 | teaspoon sugar |
| | salt and pepper to taste |
| 8 | Boston lettuce leaves, washed and dried |

Cook peas in large saucepan of boiling salted water 5 minutes. Drain and plunge into cold water. Heat butter in heavy large skillet over low heat until it begins to brown 8-10 minutes. Increase heat to medium and sauté onion until tender. Stir in peas, mint, sugar, salt and pepper to taste. Reduce heat to low and cook until peas are hot. Spoon into lettuce leaves and serve immediately. Serves 4.

*Variation: Use a can of pearl onions instead of the sliced medium onion.*

194

# Green Bean Bundles

2 pounds fresh green beans, steamed crisp-tender
6 strips bacon, partially cooked
  garlic salt to taste
4 tablespoons butter, melted
3 tablespoons packed light brown sugar

Gather 6-10 beans in bundles and wrap ½ piece of bacon around center of each bundle. Place bundles in baking dish. Sprinkle bundles with garlic salt. Pour melted butter over bundles. Sprinkle with brown sugar. Bake at 350 degrees for 15-20 minutes or until bacon is done.

*Note: Select the thinnest, most tender beans. They should be bright green and crisp. Present this do-ahead dish with any grilled meat. Serves 6*

# Spicy Black-Eyed Peas

1 (16 ounce) bag dried black-eyed peas
5 cups water
2 tablespoons minced green onions
1 tablespoon Creole seasoning
1 teaspoon dried parsley flakes
1 teaspoon garlic powder
1 teaspoon chili powder
1 teaspoon coarsely ground pepper
3 chicken-flavored bouillon cubes

Sort and wash peas; place in large Dutch oven; add water to cover peas 2 inches; let soak 8 hours. Drain peas and return to Dutch oven. Add 5 cups water and remaining ingredients. Bring to boil; cover and reduce heat; simmer 45 to 60 minutes or until tender; stirring occasionally. Serves 6-8

# Refried Beans

| | |
|---|---|
| 1 | pound dried pinto beans |
| 2 | chopped onions |
| 4 | cloves garlic, crushed |
| ⅓ | pound salt jowl |
| 1-1½ | teaspoon salt to taste |
| 1 | teaspoon chili powder |
| ¼ | teaspoon sugar |
| ¾ | teaspoon coriander |
| 1 | tablespoon garlic oil |

Soak beans overnight in water. Drain and cover with fresh water. Add garlic, 1 onion and salt jowl. Simmer covered without stirring 1½ hours. Discard salt jowl. Add salt, chili powder, sugar, coriander and garlic oil. Simmer 2 hours or until soft and juice is thickened. Mash beans with fork and stir well. Heat a small amount of cooking oil in a cast iron skillet. Sauté remaining chopped onion. Add mashed beans. Cook over medium high heat until beans start to pull away from pan. Stir occasionally (takes about 10 minutes). Serves 8

# Calico Beans

| | |
|---|---|
| ½ | pound ground beef |
| ½ | pound bacon, broken in bits |
| 1 | onion |
| ½ | cup catsup |
| ½ | cup packed brown sugar |
| 2 | tablespoons vinegar |
| 1 | large can kidney beans, drained |
| 1 | large can baked beans |
| 1 | large can butter beans, drained |

Brown in skillet beef and bacon and onion, drain. Mix catsup, brown sugar and vinegar, add to meat. Mix beans in large bowl, add to meat mixture and mix well. Bake in covered dish at 350 degrees for 1 hour. The longer they cook the better they are. Serves 10

# Praline Sweet Potato Casserole

| | | |
|---|---|---|
| 4 | cups mashed sweet potatoes | |
| 3 | tablespoons melted butter or margarine | |
| ¼ | cup brown sugar | |
| ⅓ | cup orange juice (or light cream) | |
| 1 | teaspoon brandy extract | |
| 1 | teaspoon salt | |
| 1 | teaspoon grated orange rind | |
| ½ | teaspoon ginger | |
| ⅛ | teaspoon pepper | |
| ¼ | teaspoon allspice | |
| ½ | teaspoon cinnamon | |

Combine potatoes, butter, brown sugar, orange juice, brandy, salt and spices. Mix well. Spoon into buttered 2-quart casserole or shallow baking pan. Spread topping over mixture. Bake at 350 degrees for 30 minutes.

Topping

| | | |
|---|---|---|
| ⅓ | cup brown sugar | |
| ½ | cup chopped pecans | |
| ¼ | cup melted butter | |
| ½ | teaspoon cinnamon | |

Mix sugar, pecans, cinnamon, butter. Stir until well blended. Serves 8-10

# Squash and Apple Bake

| | | |
|---|---|---|
| 2 | pounds butternut or buttercup squash | |
| ¼ | cup butter or margarine, melted | |
| 1 | teaspoon salt | |
| ½ | cup brown sugar, packed | |
| 1 | tablespoon flour | |
| ½ | teaspoon mace | |
| 2 | baking apples, cored and cut into ½ inch slices | |

Cut each squash in half. Remove seeds and fibers; pare squash. Cut into ½ inch slices. Stir together remaining ingredients, except apple slices. Arrange squash in ungreased baking dish, 11½x7½x½ inch, top with apple slices. Sprinkle sugar mixture on top: cover with foil. Bake 50-60 minutes at 350 degrees or until squash is tender. Serves 6

# Cheddar Squash Bake

| | |
|---|---|
| 2 | pounds yellow squash sliced into ½ inch slices |
| 1 | teaspoon salt |
| 1 | teaspoon sugar |
| ¾ | cup chopped onion |
| 2 | eggs, separated |
| 1 | (8 ounce) container sour cream |
| | dill weed to taste |
| | cracked pepper to taste |
| 2 | tablespoons flour |
| 2 | cups shredded cheddar cheese |
| 6 | slices bacon, cooked and crumbled |
| ⅓ | cup fine dry breadcrumbs, tossed with 1 table-spoon melted butter |

Cover squash with water. Add sugar and salt. Bring to a boil and cook about 6-8 minutes until crisp tender. Drain. Cool slightly. Beat egg yolks until thick and lemon colored; stir in sour cream and flour. Beat egg whites until stiff peaks form. Fold into yolk mixture. Layer half of squash in a lightly greased 12x8x2-inch baking dish. Sprinkle with cracked pepper and dill. Sprinkle with half of onions, egg mixture and cheese. Sprinkle with all of the bacon. Repeat layer. Sprinkle buttered breadcrumbs over top. Bake at 350 degrees for 20 minutes. Serves 8-10

# Baked Potato Fans

| | |
|---|---|
| 4 | medium potatoes |
| 1 | teaspoon salt |
| 3 | tablespoons melted butter |
| 3 | tablespoons fresh herbs, such as parsley, chives, thyme or sage |
| 4 | tablespoons grated extra sharp cheddar cheese |
| 1½ | tablespoons Parmesan cheese |

Peel potatoes if skin is tough, otherwise just scrub and rinse them. Cut potatoes into thin slices but not all the way through. Use a wooden spoon to prevent knife from cutting all the way. Put potatoes in a baking dish. Fan them slightly. Drizzle with butter. Sprinkle with herbs. Bake potatoes at 425 degrees for about 50 minutes. Remove from oven, sprinkle with cheeses. Bake potatoes for another 10-15 minutes until lightly browned, cheeses are melted and potatoes are soft inside. Serves 4

*Variation: 3 teaspoons of dried herbs for 3 tablespoons fresh herbs*

198

# Cheese Stuffed Grilled Potatoes

5    large baking potatoes
     (6 to 8 ounces each)
     cooking oil
1½   cups shredded cheddar or
     Monterey Jack cheese
½    cup light sour cream
¼-⅓  cup milk
     salt and pepper to taste

Scrub potatoes thoroughly with brush, pat dry. Rub with oil. Halve the potatoes lengthwise; wrap both halves of each potato loosely in heavy foil. Bake at 400 degrees about 1 hour or until tender. Cool slightly. Gently scoop out each potato halve leaving a ¼-inch thick shell and spooning the pulp into a large mixing bowl. (You should have about 3½-4 cups pulp.) With an electric mixer on low speed or a potato masher, beat or mash potato pulp. Add 1 cup of the cheese and sour cream; beat until smooth. If necessary, stir in enough milk to make of desired consistency. Season to taste with salt and pepper. Spoon mashed potato mixture into potato shells. Place in a greased 13x9x2-inch baking pan. (Can cover and freeze at this point.) Bake; uncovered at 425 degrees about 25 minutes or until the surface is light brown. Sprinkle with remaining cheese. Serves 10.

*Variation: Grill foil wrapped potatoes directly over medium hot coals for 45-50 minutes or until tender, turning potatoes occasionally. Or directly in coals and check after 30 minutes. To finish on grill cover the pan with foil and grill directly over medium hot coals about 25 minutes or until heated through. Sprinkle with remaining cheese.*

# Mediterranean Rice Pilaf

| | | |
|---|---|---|
| 1 | tablespoon olive oil |
| ½ | cup chopped onion |
| 1-2 | cloves garlic chopped |
| 1 | carrot, diced |
| ¼ | cup wheat berries |
| ½ | cup wild rice |
| ½ | brown rice or pilaf mixture |
| 1 | (14½ ounce) can chicken broth |
| 1 | cup water (you may need to add more) |
| | zest of one orange |
| ½ | cup sliced mushrooms (or a small can stems and pieces) |
| ½ | cup raisins or currants |
| ½ | cup almonds, chopped |
| ½ | teaspoon cinnamon |

Sauté onions, garlic and carrot in olive oil until onions are slightly translucent, do not over cook. Add rice and wheat berries, brown slightly (3 minutes). Add chicken broth and water. Cook until rice is nearly done and then add orange zest, mushrooms, currants, almonds, and cinnamon. Cook another 10 minutes. Serves 10-12

# Garlic Mashed Potatoes

| | | |
|---|---|---|
| 4 | pounds potatoes, peeled, cut into 1 inch chunks |
| 2 | teaspoons salt |
| 5 | cloves garlic, roasted |
| 1 | cup skim milk, heated |
| ½ | cup nonfat sour cream |
| 1 | tablespoon extra virgin olive oil |

In large saucepan, bring potatoes, 1 teaspoon of the salt and cold water to cover to a boil; boil for 15 minutes, until tender. Drain. Return potatoes to sauce pan, shake over high heat 30 seconds to dry. Add remaining salt and rest of ingredients. Mash to desired texture. Serves 10

200

# Ants on a Log

| | |
|---|---|
| 4 | stalks celery hearts |
| ¾ | cup peanut butter (chunky or smooth blends) |
| ½ | cup raisins |

Slice celery hearts into thirds. Fill each heart with peanut butter and place 4 or 5 raisins on top of peanut butter. Serves 12

*Apple halves can be used in place of celery.*

# Broccoli Supreme

| | |
|---|---|
| 2-3 | packages frozen broccoli (spears or chopped) precooked and drained |
| 1 | stick margarine |
| ½ | cup chopped onion |
| 1 | can cream of celery soup |
| ½ | soup can water |
| 1 | cup fresh bread crumbs |
| 1 | roll garlic cheese |
| 1 | can sliced mushrooms, drained |
| | salt and pepper to taste |
| | few drops of Worcestershire sauce |

Sauté onion in margarine. Add celery soup and water. Simmer 15 minutes. Add cheese (cut in chunks) and mushrooms. Stir until cheese is melted. Add ½ of bread crumbs and few drops of Worcestershire sauce. If using chopped broccoli, add drained broccoli and pour into 13x9 inch casserole pan. If using broccoli spears, lay cooked spears in bottom of pan, then pour sauce over broccoli. Sprinkle with remaining bread crumbs. Bake at 350 degrees for 10 minutes. Serves 8-10

*You may use 1 (4 ounce) jar of American cheese spread and garlic powder instead of the cheese roll.*

201

# Dirty Rice

½ pound lean ground beef
½ pound lean ground pork
½ cup chopped onion
½ cup chopped celery
½ cup chopped fresh parsley
¼ cup chopped green bell pepper
¼ cup chopped red bell pepper
¼ cup chopped yellow bell pepper
½ teaspoon minced garlic
8 cups cooked rice
salt to taste

In a large, deep saucepan over medium heat, sauté the ground beef and pork until crumbly. Add onions, celery, and parsley. Cook until onions are clear. Stir in bell peppers, garlic, and rice. Add salt, then mix everything well. Cook, stirring occasionally, for about 20 minutes. Reduce the heat to low, cover, and cook 1 hour. Serves 10

*You may use this to stuff 1 large hen or 8 to 10 bell peppers.*

# Butternut Squash and Fruit

2 pounds butternut squash (1 large squash) pared and seeded, and cut in chunks
1 large package dried mixed fruit (e.g. apricots, prunes, apples, etc.)
⅔ cup apple juice or water
½ teaspoon cinnamon

Spray baking dish with nonstick cooking spray. Put in squash chunks. Add dried fruit. Pour liquid over all. Sprinkle with cinnamon. Cover and bake 1 hour at 375 degrees. Serves 6.

*You can use 2 peeled, sliced apples instead of dried fruit. Reduce liquid to ½ cup if you do this. You can also use 2 apples and ½ cup raisins and ⅔ cup liquid.*
*This is good with pork. Children seem to prefer apples and raisins, but adults seem to enjoy the mixed fruit.*

202

# Asparagus Parmigiano

| | |
|---|---|
| 1½ | pounds fresh asparagus, or 2 packages frozen |
| 1 | onion, chopped |
| 2 | garlic, cloves, minced |
| 3 | tablespoons olive oil |
| ¼ | teaspoon hot pepper sauce |
| 1 | (28 ounce) can whole tomatoes |
| ½ | teaspoon thyme |
| 1 | (16 ounce) can thick tomato sauce |
| ½ | pound mozzarella cheese grated Parmesan cheese |

Steam asparagus for 7 minutes. Drain asparagus; arrange in shallow baking dish.

Sauté onion and garlic in oil until golden. Add hot pepper sauce and tomatoes. Simmer, uncovered for 10 minutes. Add thyme and tomato sauce; simmer for 20 minutes longer.

Pour sauce over asparagus. Place slices of mozzarella cheese on top. Sprinkle with Parmesan cheese. Bake at 350 degrees for 30 minutes or until cheese is browned.

# Bleu Cheese Asparagus

| | |
|---|---|
| 1½ | pound fresh asparagus vegetable cooking spry |
| 2 | teaspoons reduced calorie margarine |
| 2 | tablespoons cider vinegar |
| 3 | tablespoons crumbled bleu cheese |
| 2 | tablespoons chopped pecans, roasted |

Snap off tough ends of asparagus. Remove scales from stalks with a knife or vegetable peeler if desired.

Coat a large nonstick skillet with cooking spray; add margarine. Place over medium heat until margarine melts. Add asparagus and sauté 3 to 4 minutes. Add vinegar; cover and simmer 2 or 3 minutes or until asparagus is crisp tender. Add bleu cheese and chopped pecans; toss gently. Serve warm. Serves 6

# Black Beans Cilantro

| | | |
|---|---|---|
| 1 | pound dry black beans | |
| 2 | quarts chicken stock | |
| ¼ | cup olive oil | |
| 1 | onion, chopped | |
| 5 | cloves garlic, chopped | |
| 2 | fresh hot chilies, seeded and chopped | |
| ¼ | cup fresh parsley, chopped | |
| ½ | cup fresh cilantro, chopped | |

Rinse dried black beans with cold water in strainer. In large stock pot, combine chicken stock, beans and olive oil. Slow boil until stock starts to turn black, approximately 2 hours. Add onion, garlic, chilies, parsley and cilantro. Continue to slow boil until beans are tender and stock is slightly thick.

Serve with a combination of sour cream, grated Monterey Jack and cheddar cheese, salsa and chopped cilantro. Also good over rice.

Desserts

# Cherry Bisque Tortoni

2 egg whites
2 tablespoons sugar
⅓ cup nutty barley cereal
¼ cup almonds, coarsely chopped
¼ cup maraschino cherries, quartered
1 tablespoon cherry juice
½ teaspoon vanilla
1 cup whipping cream, whipped
¼ cup powdered sugar
½ cup additional grapenuts

Beat egg whites until foamy. Add 2 tablespoon sugar and beat until stiff.

Mix together cereal, almonds, cherries, cherry juice, vanilla, whipped cream and powdered sugar. Fold into egg white mixture.

Sprinkle some cereal into bottom of cupcake liners, spoon in filling and top with cereal. Freeze until ready to serve. Serves 8

*Especially pretty in foil cupcake liners.*

# Date Bars

8 ounces chopped dates
½ cup sugar
½ cup water
1 cup nuts, chopped
2 cups oatmeal
2 cups brown sugar
2 cups flour
2 sticks corn oil margarine
1 teaspoon soda dissolved in ¾ teaspoon hot water
½ teaspoon salt

In small pan cook dates, sugar, water and nuts until thick. Set aside to cool while mixing dough. Mix oatmeal, brown sugar, flour and salt in large bowl. Using a large wooden spoon, cut in margarine. Finish mixing with fingers and pour in soda water.

Pat half of the dough in a greased and floured 9x13-inch pan. Spread filling with wooded spoon on top of dough. Pat the rest of the dough on top of the date filling.

Cook 30 minutes at 350 degrees. Don't overcook. Cut into bars after partly cool. Serves 30

# Toffee

1 pound butter (no substitute)
2 cups sugar
6 ounces blanched slivered almonds
1 half pound chocolate bar, grated
6 ounces almonds, finely chopped in blender

Melt butter in heavy saucepan. Turn heat on high and add sugar, stirring constantly with wooden spoon. Add blanched almonds and cook to 300 degrees (hard crack). Pour onto jelly roll pan. Sprinkle with grated chocolate and smooth over toffee. Add finely chopped almonds, press to hold.

*Good for Christmas gifts.*

# Triple Treat Mint Bars

Base
½ cup butter, melted
¼ cup granulated sugar
⅓ cup cocoa
1 egg
2 cups graham cracker crumbs
1 cup flaked coconut
½ cup pecans or walnuts, chopped

Filling
¼ cup butter
2 tablespoons custard powder
1 teaspoon peppermint extract
green food coloring
3 tablespoons milk
2 cups powdered sugar, sifted

Icing
3 ounces semi-sweet chocolate
1½ tablespoons butter

Mix together ½ cup melted butter, granulated sugar, cocoa, egg, graham cracker crumbs, flaked coconut and nuts. Press into a 9x10-inch pan. Refrigerate while making filling.

For filling, cream together ¼ cup butter, custard powder, mint extract, and green food coloring for desired tint. Gradually blend in milk and powdered sugar alternately. Spread on base in pan. Chill well before icing.

For icing, melt chocolate and butter together. Spread on chilled mixture and chill until chocolate sets.

Cut into bars. Store in refrigerator.

# White Chocolate Chunk Macadamia Nut Cookies

| | |
|---|---|
| 1 | cup butter |
| 1 | cup light brown sugar, firmly packed |
| ½ | cup sugar |
| 2 | eggs |
| 1 | teaspoon vanilla |
| 2¼ | cup flour |
| 1 | teaspoon baking soda |
| 1 | teaspoon salt |
| 1 | cup macadamia nuts, coarsely chopped |
| 2 | cups white chocolate, broken into bite-sized chunks |

Cream butter and sugars until light and fluffy. Beat in eggs and vanilla.

Combine flour, soda, and salt; gradually add to creamed mixture. Stir in nuts and chocolate.

Drop by heaping tablespoonfuls onto greased baking sheets. Bake in preheated 350-degree oven for 10 to 12 minutes. Cool slightly before removing from baking sheet. Makes approximately 6 dozen

# Crispy Oat Cookies

| | |
|---|---|
| 1 | cup butter or margarine, softened |
| 1 | cup sugar |
| 1 | cup firmly packed brown sugar |
| 1 | egg |
| 1 | cup vegetable oil |
| 1 | teaspoon vanilla |
| 3½ | cups all purpose flour |
| 1 | teaspoon soda |
| ½ | teaspoon salt |
| 1 | cup regular oats, un-cooked |
| 1 | cup crushed corn flakes |
| ½ | cup flaked coconut |
| ½ | cup walnuts or pecans, chopped |

Cream butter, gradually add sugars and beat well. Add egg and beat. Mix in oil and vanilla. Combine flour, soda, and salt and add to creamed mixture, mixing well. Add oats and remaining ingredients.

Shape dough into one-inch balls. Place on an ungreased baking sheet and flatten with tines of a fork. Bake at 325 degrees for 15 minutes. Cool slightly, remove from cookie sheets and cool. Makes 8 to 10 dozen

# Chocolate Cinnamon Biscotti

1¼ cups all-purpose flour
¾ cup sugar
¼ cup cocoa
1 tablespoon ground cinnamon
¾ teaspoon baking powder
¼ teaspoon ground nutmeg
⅛ teaspoon salt
½ stick butter or margarine, softened
2 egg whites
½ teaspoon almond extract
¼ cup sliced toasted almonds
¼ cup dried cranberries or cherries
1 additional egg white and 1 teaspoon sugar

Preheat oven to 350 degrees. Grease large baking sheet and set aside.

In large mixing bowl, combine flour, ¾ cup sugar, cocoa, cinnamon, baking powder, nutmeg and salt. Using an electric mixer on medium speed, beat in butter or margarine until mixture resembles coarse crumbs. Add 2 egg whites and almond extract. Beat about one minute until soft dough forms.

Stir in almonds and fruit. Shape dough into two logs, approximately 8x2 inches. Lightly beat remaining egg white and brush over logs. Sprinkle each log with ½ teaspoon sugar.

Bake until firm, but slightly pliable, 30-35 minutes. Using two spatulas, remove to wire rack, set baking sheet aside. Cool until logs can be handled, about 10 minutes.

Reduce oven temperature to 325 degrees and transfer logs to cutting board. Using a serrated knife, cut logs into ½-inch thick diagonal slices. Place cut side down on baking sheet. Bake until crisp, about 15 minutes.

Cool on wire rack completely before storing in an air-tight container. Makes 18-24 pieces

# Oatmeal Fudge Cookies

2 cups sugar
3 tablespoon cocoa
1 stick margarine or butter
½ cup milk
3 cups quick cooking oatmeal
½ cup peanut butter
1 teaspoon vanilla
coconut, optional

Bring sugar, cocoa, butter and milk to a boil. Boil for one minute. Take off heat and add remaining ingredients. Drop by teaspoon on waxed paper. When set up, remove to cookie jar. Makes 2 dozen

*For butterscotch cookies, omit cocoa.*

# Treasure Chest Bars

½ cup brown sugar
½ cup white sugar
½ cup margarine
2 eggs
1 teaspoon vanilla
2 cups flour
½ teaspoon baking powder
½ teaspoon salt
¾ cup milk
1 cup maraschino cherries, cut up
1 cup chocolate chips
1 cup nuts, chopped (optional)

Cream together sugars and margarine. Blend in eggs and vanilla. Add flour, baking powder and salt, alternately with milk and blend well.

Add maraschino cherries, chocolate chips and nuts and mix.

Bake in 9x13-inch pan 25-30 minutes at 325 degrees. Cool, frost and cut into bars.

Frosting
¼ cup butter
2 cups powdered sugar
½ teaspoon vanilla
2 tablespoons milk

Brown butter in saucepan. Blend in sugar and vanilla. Add milk and beat.

210

*Photo on right ~*
Crusted Salmon with Herbed
Mayonnaise, page 160

# Best Chocolate Brownies

| | |
|---|---|
| 8 | ounces unsweetened chocolate |
| 1 | cup butter |
| 5 | eggs |
| 3 | cups sugar |
| 1 | tablespoon vanilla |
| 1½ | cups all-purpose flour |
| 2 | cups walnuts or pecans, coarsely chopped |

Melt chocolate and butter in saucepan over very low heat, stirring constantly (or heat chocolate and butter at high power in non-metal bowl in microwave for 2½ minutes, stirring after 1 minute, then stir until melted and smooth). Cool slightly.

Beat eggs, sugar, and vanilla in large mixing bowl on high speed for 10 minutes. Blend in chocolate mixture on low speed.

Add flour, beating just to blend. Stir in nuts.

Spread in greased 13x9-inch pan. Bake at 375 degrees for 35-40 minutes, do not overbake.

Cool in pan; frost and cut in squares.

### Frosting

| | |
|---|---|
| 1½ | cups sugar |
| 6 | tablespoons butter |
| 6 | tablespoons milk or half-and-half |
| 1 | cup semi-sweet chocolate chips |

Mix sugar, butter and milk in saucepan. Bring to boil stirring constantly and boil for one minute. Remove from heat and add chocolate chips. Beat until smooth (may add another tablespoon of milk if consistency is too thick). When cool, frost brownies. Makes 32 brownies

# Swedish Nut Balls

| | |
|---|---|
| 1 | cup butter, or margarine |
| ½ | cup powdered sugar |
| 1 | teaspoon vanilla |
| 2¼ | cups sifted flour |
| ½ | teaspoon salt |
| ¾ | cup chopped nuts |
| | powdered sugar |

Cream butter and sugar. Add vanilla. Add dry ingredients. Form into walnut-size balls. Bake at 400 degrees for 15 minutes. When cool, roll in powdered sugar.

*Photo on left ~*
Bloom Where You Are
Planted, page 14

211

## Meringue Cookies

2   egg whites
¾   cup sugar (extra fine, if
      possible)
½   cup chopped walnuts
½   cup chocolate bits

Beat egg whites until stiff. Beat in sugar one tablespoon at a time, beating very well after each addition. Line cookie sheet with foil. Drop egg white mixture on cookie sheet using approximately 1 round tablespoon per cookie. Preheat oven to 350 degrees. Put meringue in oven. Turn oven off immediately. Leave in oven overnight or approximately 8 hours. Serves 20

*Especially nice to use during the Christmas Holidays.*

## CWC Chocolate Chip Cookies

1   cup butter
1   cup sugar
1   cup brown sugar
2   eggs
1   teaspoon vanilla
2   cups flour
1   teaspoon baking soda
2¼  cups oatmeal
1   teaspoon baking powder
½   teaspoon salt
12  ounces chocolate chips
1   (4 ounce) milk chocolate
      bar, grated
1½  cups chopped pecans

Measure oatmeal and blend in blender to a fine powder (will make 2½ cups blended oatmeal).

Cream the butter and both sugars. Add eggs and vanilla; mix together with flour, baking soda, oatmeal, baking powder and salt. Add chocolate chips, grated chocolate bar, and nuts.

Roll into balls and place two inches apart on a cookie sheet.

Bake for 10 minutes at 375 degrees. Makes 5 dozen cookies.

# Gourmet Chocolate Chip Cookies

| | |
|---|---|
| 1 | cup butter |
| ¾ | cup sugar |
| ¾ | cup brown sugar |
| 1 | tablespoon vanilla |
| 1 | tablespoon Frangelico |
| 1 | tablespoon Kahlúa |
| 2 | eggs |
| 2½ | cups flour |
| 1 | teaspoon baking soda |
| ½ | teaspoon salt |
| 1 | (12 ounce) package milk chocolate chips |
| 1 | (12 ounce) package semi-sweet chocolate chips |
| ½ | cup walnuts, chopped |
| ½ | cup pecans, chopped |
| ½ | cup macadamia nuts, chopped |

Preheat oven to 325. Beat first six ingredients until light and fluffy. Add eggs, beat well. Mix flour, soda, salt; stir in butter mixture. Mix in chips and nuts. Drop batter by ¼ cupfuls onto ungreased cookie sheet. Bake 15 minutes until golden brown.

# Dottie's Sinful Fruit Dip

| | |
|---|---|
| 1 | (8 ounce) package cream cheese |
| 1 | (3 ounce) package cream cheese |
| 1 | (7 ounce) jar marshmallow cream |
| 1 | cup sifted powdered sugar |
| 1 | (8 ounce) carton sour cream |
| 2 | teaspoons vanilla |
| 2 | teaspoons almond extract |
| 2 | tablespoons cognac |

Bring cream cheese to room temperature. With electric mixer combine cream cheese with other ingredients and beat until smooth.

*Great for strawberries or green apples. Can be prepared ahead.*

# Pavlova

6 egg whites
½ teaspoon salt
½ teaspoon vanilla
2 teaspoons white vinegar
1½ cups granulated sugar
1 teaspoon cornstarch
½ pint whipped cream,
  whipped
  fruit for garnish, such as
    strawberries, kiwi, or
    peaches

Heat oven to 250 degrees. Place grease proof paper on a cold oven tray.

Beat egg whites to a soft foam. Add salt, vanilla and vinegar, continue beating for a short time until moderately stiff foam is formed. Add ¼ of sugar and beat for a short time. Repeat two more times. Mix remaining sugar with cornstarch and add as above. Finish beating until the mixture forms standing peaks which just fold slightly at the tips when the beater is lifted from the mixture.

Heap on the waxed paper. Make them in individual sizes mounding up the sides. They can be made in one large size, but it may be hard to slice and serve that way. Bake for 1½ to 2 hours on lower oven rack.

Place whipped cream in indentation an hour or so before serving. Place in refrigerator. Top with fresh fruit when serving.

*Color of cooked Pavlova should be a very pale fawn and the texture of the center resembles marshmallows. If possible the cake should be cooled in the oven with the door open.*
*Place whipped cream in indentation an hour or so before serving - place in refrigerator. When ready to serve place fresh fruit on whipped cream. Almost any kind of fruit is great. Kiwi and berries are very typical.*

*(continued on next page)*

*Then put a dollop of whipped cream on top.*

*Eggs a few days old at room temperature are best for making Marshmallow Pavlova. In method where whites are beaten first and sugar added gradually, beat whites firm before adding sugar. Salt is used to strengthen and stabilize egg whites helping them to hold their aerated volume.*

*Granulated sugar gives a firmer result. Be sure all sugar is dissolved, otherwise the undissolved sugar will melt during cooking and give a "weepy" sticky Pavlova. To test if sugar is dissolved, rub a little of the mixture between fingers. In classic Pavlova the last quantity of sugar is mixed with the cornstarch and just lightly folded in at the last minute. The cornstarch prevents sugar "weeping". This method gives a very characteristic Pavlova - crisp and crunchy on the outside, with soft marshmallow center. Cornstarch helps to dry out Pavlova, the more cornstarch used, the drier the Pavlova will be. Vinegar helps form the marshmallow center and also whitens the Pavlova.*

*Aluminum foil is excellent to cover the baking tray a well as waxed paper or brown paper or parchment. Marshmallow Pavlova is best stored in airtight tin in refrigerator - 2 days okay.*

# Venetian Strawberries

1    pound large fresh straw-
     berries
2    teaspoons white vinegar
½    cup brown sugar
     freshly ground black
     pepper to taste
2    tablespoons Cointreau
     liqueur

Wash strawberries and set aside to get fruit room temperature, about 30 minutes before slicing berries in 4 sections and placing in a large bowl. Lace strawberries with vinegar and toss berries several times. Add sugar and toss again to reduce sugar to a syrup. Sprinkle freshly ground pepper on mixture and toss again.

Lace berries with liqueur and set aside 15 minutes before serving. Serves 6

# Fruit Pizza

1    roll sugar cookie dough
     (store bought)
1    (8 ounce) cream cheese,
     softened
¼    cup granulated sugar
¼    cup pineapple juice
1    teaspoon vanilla
2    kiwi, sliced
1    pint strawberries, sliced
1    banana, sliced
2    medium peaches, sliced
½    pint blueberries
½    pint raspberries

Press cookie dough into a ten inch tart pan. Bake at 350 degrees for 12-15 minutes. Let cool. Cream together cream cheese, sugar, pineapple juice and vanilla. Spread over crust. Place fruit in rows in a circular pattern on top of cream cheese so that when it is sliced all the different fruits are on each slice. Chill for ½ hour and slice.

# Caramel Bananas

| | |
|---|---|
| 4 | large bananas |
| ¾ | cup firmly packed light brown sugar |
| 4 | tablespoons unsalted butter |
| ¾ | cup whipping cream, divided |

Peel bananas, split lengthwise and place in a serving dish. Cook sugar, 3 tablespoons of the cream and butter until thickened, about 5 minutes. Add vanilla and pour while hot over bananas. Whip remainder of cream. When bananas and sauce cool, cover with whipped cream and serve immediately, sprinkled with chopped nuts, if desired. Serves 4-8

*The sauce is also excellent on vanilla ice cream or frozen yogurt.*

# Petit Pots de Crème au Chocolat (Little Chocolate Pots)

| | |
|---|---|
| 1 | (6 ounce) package of semi-sweet chocolate chips |
| 1 | whole egg |
| | pinch salt |
| 2 | tablespoons sugar |
| ¾ | cup (6 ounces) of cream, half-and-half or milk |
| 2 | tablespoons of rum, liquor or 1 teaspoon vanilla |

Put all ingredients except cream and rum or vanilla in blender. Pulse a couple of times to get things mixed up. Heat cream until just boiling (about 2 minutes in microwave on high). With blender running, add hot cream. (This "cooks" the egg and melts the chocolate.) Blend one full minute. Add rum or vanilla and blend to mix. Pour into pots de crème cups, half cup ramekins or demitasse cups. Refrigerate. Add decorations before serving. Serves 4-6

*Bar chocolate (well chopped) can be used instead of chips. Garnish with a dollop of whipped cream or a twist of orange peel or a whole raspberry. Use raspberry or grand marnier as substitute for rum.*

# Cream Puffs

½ cup water
¼ cup butter
½ cup all-purpose flour
2 eggs

Heat oven to 400 degrees. Heat water and butter to rolling boil in a sauce-pan. Stir in flour. Stir vigorously over low heat until mixture forms a ball, about 1 minute. Remove from heat. Beat in eggs, all at once and continue beating until smooth. Drop dough by scant ¼ cupfuls about 3 inches apart onto ungreased cookie sheet. Bake until puffed and golden, 35 to 40 minutes. Cool away from draft.

When ready to serve: Cut off tops; pull out any filaments of soft dough. Fill puffs with ice cream replace top and drizzle with chocolate sauce.

# Fabulous 'N Easy Chocolate Filling

1 cup or 6 ounces quality semi-sweet chocolate (morsels or baking chocolate)
3 tablespoons whole milk
2 tablespoons granulated sugar
4 eggs
1 teaspoon vanilla

Place chocolate pieces, milk and sugar in a microwave safe 4 cup glass measuring cup. Microwave on full power approximately 1 minute. Stir until mixture is smooth and well blended. Microwave a few additional seconds if necessary. Can also be melted conventionally over boiling water. Set aside to cool.

Meanwhile, separate eggs. Add egg yolks, one at a time, to the cooled mixture, beating well after each addition. Stir in vanilla.

In a large bowl, beat room tempera-ture egg whites until stiff. Carefully fold egg whites into chocolate mixture until no streaks of white remain. Serves 8 (one pie)

*(continued on next page)*

218

*Pie: Pour into a 9-inch baked pie shell or graham cracker or chocolate cookie pie shell. Decorate with lightly sweetened whipped cream. Refrigerate until ready to serve.*
*Mousse: Place in individual serving dishes. Decorate with whipped cream.*
*A spectacular dessert: Baste and soak 8 stemmed maraschino cherries in 3 tablespoons rum for 15 minutes. Place in freezer. Make filling doubling recipe. Melt chocolate without milk or sugar. Stir until smooth. Dip each chilled cherry in chocolate to coat. Place on waxed paper. Add milk and sugar to remaining melted chocolate; microwave briefly to warm; stir until smooth. Proceed with recipe. Place ladyfingers side by side to line springform pan sides. Cover bottom, cutting ladyfingers to cover evenly. Sprinkle bottom ladyfingers lightly with leftover rum. Add half of chocolate mixture, then a second layer of ladyfingers, sprinkle with rum, then remaining chocolate mixture. Refrigerate at least 2 hours.*
*To serve, carefully slide knife around pan; remove collar. Lightly dust top and sides with confectionery sugar. Decorate with sweetened whipped cream and garnish with chocolate dipped cherries.*
*This has been a family "chocolate pie" recipe for more than 50 years. Not a cream pie and not French silk, it has an intense chocolate flavor that is smooth and light. Through the years, in duplicating this recipe, I have discovered the filling's versatility. In addition to pies, I have filled cream horns, meringues, tarts and tulles. This filling does not become watery in the refrigerator and does not break down quickly at room temperature. Refrigerated, it remains fresh and delicious, even over several days. Best of all it is quick, inexpensive and easy to prepare.*

# Strawberry Meringues

3    egg whites
1    teaspoon vanilla
½    teaspoon cream of tartar
    salt
1    cup granulated sugar
1    pint strawberries
2    ounces semisweet choco-
      late (2 squares)
2    teaspoons butter
1    cup whipping cream
2    tablespoons powdered
      sugar

Place egg whites in small mixing bowl; let stand at room temperature about 1 hour. Cover baking sheets with brown paper. Draw eight 3-inch circles on the brown paper.

For meringue, combine egg whites, vanilla, cream of tartar and salt. Beat until soft peaks form. Gradually add a cup of granulated sugar, beating until stiff peaks form. Spread meringue over the 8 circles, using about ⅓ cup for each. Using the back of a spoon, shape into shells.

Bake at 275 degrees for 1 hour. For crisper meringue shells turn off oven; dry meringue shells in oven with door closed about 1 hour. Peel off brown paper.

Halve strawberries; sweeten with a little granulated sugar, if desired. Melt chocolate and butter; cool. Combine whipping cream and powdered sugar; beat until stiff peaks form.

To assemble drizzle about 1 teaspoon of the cooled chocolate mixture over each shell. Reserve about ½ cup of the whipped cream for garnish; divide remainder evenly among the shells. Top with the halved strawberries. Garnish with reserved whipped cream. Serves 8

# Fruit Curd Tartlets

1 cup flour
¼ cup ground nuts (walnuts, almonds or pistachios, etc.)
½ teaspoon salt
⅓ cup (5⅓ tablespoons) cold unsalted butter, cut into 8 pieces
2 tablespoons water
1¼ cups fruit curds, preferably of different flavors such as lemon and orange
¼ cup finely chopped nuts

Combine flour, ground nuts and salt in a mixing bowl or the bowl of a food processor. Add butter and cut in by hand or process briefly until mixture resembles course crumbs. Sprinkle with 2 tablespoons cold water and toss with a fork or pulse quickly in processor. Add additional water by teaspoonful, if necessary, until dough is moist enough to hold together. Gather into a ball, flatten into a circle , and wrap in plastic wrap. Chill in refrigerator for 45 minutes.

On a lightly floured surface, roll out dough about ⅛ inch thick. Cut dough to fit 18 each 1½-inch to 2-inch tartlet molds (or miniature muffin cups). Ease dough into molds and press gently into corners and sides. Prick surfaces with a fork. Chill tartlets on a baking sheet for about 20 minutes.

Bake in center of oven for 8-10 minutes at 450 until lightly colored and let cool slightly in molds. Carefully invert and cool completely on a wire rack.

An hour or so before serving, spoon 1-2 teaspoons fruit curd into each pastry shell. Sprinkle the top of each with a few chopped nuts (to match nuts in dough).

221

# Flan

½ cup sugar
1 (14 ounce) can sweetened condensed milk
14 ounces milk
1 teaspoon vanilla
4 eggs

Preheat oven to 350 degrees. Fill a 9x13x2-inch glass baking pan half full of tap water and set aside. Heat a large (at least 12 inch) non-stick skillet at medium-high heat until hot. Add the sugar. Stir constantly. Sugar will begin to melt, continue to stir until sugar is all melted and slightly brown in color. Don't leave it on too long or it will start to smoke and burn! Immediately pour into one quart glass baking dish. Use a rubber spatula to scrape all the sugar from the skillet into the baking dish.

Add entire can of sweetened condensed milk (scraping can with spatula to get it all) to blender container. Refill condensed milk can with milk and add to the blender along with vanilla and eggs. Blend well. Pour into baking dish on top of caramelized sugar.

Set baking dish into 9x13-inch pan and place in oven. (This prevents the custard from overcooking or burning.) Bake for one hour. Remove from oven and allow to cool at least 1 hour before placing in refrigerator.

To serve: Run a knife around the edges of the baking dish and invert onto plate. Serve each slice caramelized sugar side up, with an extra spoonful of "sauce" from dish.

*Kahlúa Flan - Follow directions above, except: After pouring caramelized sugar into baking dish, pour*

*(continued on next page)*

*(Flan continued)*

*¼ cup of Kahlúa on top before the milk mixture or add ¼ cup of Kahlúa to the sweetened condensed milk can before filling the rest of the way with milk (substitutes as part of the milk).*

## Mango Raspberry Brûlée

| | |
|---|---|
| 5 | egg yolks |
| 2 | cups heavy cream |
| ⅔ | cup half-and-half |
| 2 | cups sugar, divided |
| ½ | teaspoon vanilla extract |
| 1 | cup mango, chopped into ¼ inch cubes |
| 1½ | cups raspberries |
| | hot water |

Preheat oven to 325 degrees. In a large bowl, lightly whip the egg yolks. Add the cream, half-and-half, ⅓ cup plus 1 tablespoon sugar, and vanilla. Blend well.

Distribute combined fruits evenly between the ramekins. Pour the custard evenly over the fruit. Set the ramekins in a pan with at least 2 inch sides and fill the pan with hot water reaching halfway up the sides of the ramekins. Bake for 30 to 40 minutes or until the custard is softly set.

Remove from oven and let sit in hot water for 20 minutes. Then place on rack to cool. At this point the brûlées may be refrigerated for use later that day, or overnight.

To serve the brûlees, sprinkle each ramekin with 1 to 2 tablespoons sugar and place under broiler until caramelized. Rotate the ramekins as necessary. The caramelization process is complete when dark golden hard-crack surface is formed. The brûlées should not be caramelized more than 30 minutes in advance of serving or the sugar will melt. Serves 6

# Napoleons

1 package puff pastry sheets
1 recipe Napoleon filling
   (recipe follows)
   chocolate frosting (mix,
      canned, or from
      scratch)

Thaw pastry sheets according to package directions; preheat oven to 375 degrees. Trim edges (so it will rise evenly); cut each sheet into 6 large or approximately 24 smaller pastries. Place on ungreased baking sheet and bake at 375 degrees until pastries puff up and are lightly browned approximately 10-15 minutes. Cool on wire rack. When pastries have cooled, split in half lengthwise. Spread Napoleon filling on bottom half of each pastry and replace the top. Gently spread each top with chocolate frosting. Chill. Will keep in refrigerator for two to three days.

Best served when chilled or the next day (pastries will soften if refrigerated longer).

## Napoleon Filling

1 cup granulated sugar
¼ cup cornstarch
3 cups milk
2 teaspoons vanilla extract
¼ cup all purpose flour
½ teaspoon salt
4 beaten egg yolks

In saucepan combine sugar, flour, cornstarch, and salt. Stir in milk. Cook, stirring constantly until mixture thickens and bubbles. Stir a little of the hot mixture into egg yolks; return to hot mixture in saucepan. Bring just to boiling, stirring constantly. Cool; stir in vanilla extract. Chill. Beat until smooth just before filling napoleons. Serves 6-24 depending on size

*Small ones are easily carried to party or dinner for finger-food type dessert.*

# Pumpkin Cheesecake with Frangelico

24 gingersnaps
3 tablespoons sugar
¼ cup unsalted butter, melted
2 (8 ounce) packages cream cheese, room temperature
1 (16 ounce) can solid pack pumpkin
5 eggs, room temperature
¾ cup brown sugar firmly packed
½ cup Frangelico
1 teaspoon cinnamon
1 teaspoon vanilla
¼ teaspoon ground ginger
⅛ teaspoon grated nutmeg
⅛ teaspoon ground cloves

Topping
1 (16 ounce) carton sour cream
¼ cup sugar
¼ cup Frangelico
10-12 hazelnuts

Crust: Grind gingersnaps with sugar in food processor to fine crumbs. With machine running, slowly add butter. Press mixture onto bottom of 9 inch springform pan. Freeze for 15 minutes. (May be prepared two days ahead).

Filling: Position rack in center of oven and preheat to 350 degrees. Blend all ingredients in processor until smooth, stopping once to scrape down sides of work bowl. Pour filling into crust lined pan. Bake until edges of cake begin to pull away from sides of pan and cake begins to brown, about 45 minutes, center will not be firm.

Whisk together sour cream, sugar, and Frangelico. Without removing cake from oven, pour topping evenly over hot cake starting at edges. Spread evenly. Continue baking cake until edges begin to bubble, about 10 minutes. Cool on rack. Refrigerate at least 12 hours. (May be prepared 2 days ahead.) Lightly press hazelnuts into top edge of cake. Let stand at room temperature for 40 minutes before serving.

# Mocha-Orange Cheesecake Royale

**Crust**

| | |
|---|---|
| 10 | ounces orange flavored cookies, broken into pieces (about 21 cookies) |
| ¼ | cup (½ stick) unsalted butter, cut into pieces |
| 1½ | teaspoons instant espresso powder |

**Filling**

| | |
|---|---|
| 4 | ounces bittersweet or semi-sweet chocolate, chopped |
| 2 | (8 ounce) packages cream cheese, room temperature |
| ¾ | cup sugar |
| ⅓ | cup frozen orange juice concentrate, thawed |
| 2 | tablespoons coffee liqueur |
| 2 | tablespoons orange liqueur |
| 2 | tablespoons instant espresso powder |
| 3 | large eggs |

**Topping**

| | |
|---|---|
| 1½ | cups sour cream |
| 6 | tablespoons packed powdered sugar |
| 4 | teaspoons instant espresso powder |
| | orange slices (optional) |
| | chocolate curls (optional) |

Crust: Preheat oven to 325 degrees. Combine all ingredients in processor. Process until moist crumbs form. Press crumbs onto bottom and sides of prepared 9 inch springform pan with 2¼ inch high sides. Bake crust until puffed and brown, about 15 minutes. Cool. Maintain oven temperature.

Filling: Melt chocolate in top of a double boiler set over simmering water, stirring until smooth. Using electric mixer, beat cream cheese and sugar in large bowl until smooth. Mix in melted chocolate. Add juice concentrate, liqueurs and espresso. Beat until mixture is smooth. Beat in eggs, adding them one at a time.

Spoon ⅓ cup batter into pastry bag fitted with a ¼-inch plain tip. Chill. Pour remaining batter into crust. Bake until softly set in center and slightly puffed at edges, about 45 minutes. Let cool 10 minutes. Maintain oven temperature.

Topping: Mix sour cream, powdered sugar and espresso powder in small bowl until espresso powder dissolves. Spread over hot cake. Pipe reserved ⅓ cup cake batter in parallel stripes (about ½ inch apart) over topping.

Bake cake until topping is set, about 5 minutes. Cut around pan sides to

*(continued on next page)*

226

loosen crust. Place cake immediately into refrigerator. Chill completely, about 8 hours.

Cut around pan sides and release. Top with oranges and chocolate if desired.

# Chocolate Amaretto Cheesecake

Crust

|       |                                                      |
|-------|------------------------------------------------------|
| 1½    | cups chocolate wafer crumbs                          |
| 1     | cup blanched almonds, lightly toasted and chopped    |
| ⅓     | cup sugar                                            |
| 6     | tablespoons butter, softened                         |

Filling and Topping

|       |                                                        |
|-------|--------------------------------------------------------|
| 3     | (8 ounce) packages cream cheese, softened              |
| 1     | cup sugar                                              |
| 4     | eggs, room temperature                                 |
| ⅓     | cup heavy cream                                        |
| ¼     | cup Amaretto liqueur                                   |
| 1     | teaspoon vanilla                                       |
| 2     | cups sour cream                                        |
| 1     | tablespoon sugar                                       |
| 1     | teaspoon vanilla                                       |
| ½     | cup blanched almonds, lightly toasted and chopped      |

Crust: Combine chocolate wafer crumbs, almonds, sugar and butter in bowl and mix well. Pat mixture onto the bottom of buttered 9 inch spring-form pan.

Filling and Topping: In large bowl, cream together cream cheese and 1 cup sugar. Beat in eggs, one at a time, beating well after each addition. Add heavy cream, Amaretto and 1 teaspoon vanilla and beat until light and fluffy.

Pour mixture into crust and bake at 375 degrees for 30 minutes. Let stand for 5 minutes.

Combine sour cream, 1 tablespoon sugar and 1 teaspoon vanilla. Spread mixture evenly on cake and bake 5 minutes more. Cool completely and chill overnight.

Remove sides of pan and press slivered almonds (lightly toasted) around the top outside edge.

# Almond Candy Bar Cheesecake

**Crust**

1½  cups graham cracker crumbs

1½  cups sweetened flaked coconut, toasted

½  cup (2 ounces) sliced almonds, toasted

¼  cup sugar

½  cup (1 stick) unsalted butter, melted

**Filling**

4  (8 ounce) packages cream cheese, room temperature

1  cup sugar

4  large eggs

1  cup sweetened flaked coconut, toasted

1  tablespoon coconut extract

1  cup sliced almonds, toasted

**Glaze**

1  cup semisweet chocolate chips

¾  cup whipping cream

1½  teaspoon vanilla extract

Crust: Preheat oven to 350 degrees. Wrap outside of 9-inch diameter springform pan with 2¾ inch high sides with foil.

Finely grind cracker crumbs, coconut, almonds and sugar in processor. Add butter. Process until moist crumbs form. Press mixture onto bottom and 1 inch up sides of pan. Bake crust until set and beginning to brown, about 12 minutes. Cool. Reduce oven to 325 degrees.

Filling: Using electric mixer, beat cream cheese and sugar in large bowl until smooth. Add eggs one at a time, beating until blended after each addition. Mix in coconut and extract. Fold in almonds. Transfer filling to crust. Bake at 325 degrees until cake is puffed and no longer moves when pan is shaken, about 1 hour and 15 minutes. Cool completely on rack.

Glaze: Combine 1 cup chocolate chips, cream and vanilla in small saucepan. Stir over medium low heat until smooth. Cool until glaze begins to thicken but can still be poured, about 30 minutes. Pour glaze over cooled cake, spreading evenly. Chill overnight. Run knife around edge of pan. Release side. Serves 10-12

*Begin a day ahead.*

# Chocolate Raspberry Cheesecake

Crust

| | |
|---|---|
| 1½ | cups crushed chocolate cookies (about 18) |
| 2 | tablespoons melted butter |

Filling

| | |
|---|---|
| 4 | (8 ounce) packages cream cheese, softened |
| 1¼ | cups sugar |
| 3 | eggs |
| 1 | cup sour cream |
| 1 | teaspoon vanilla |
| 1 | (6 ounce) package chocolate chips, melted |
| ⅓ | cup strained red raspberry preserves |
| 1 | (6 ounce) package chocolate chips |
| ¼ | cup whipping cream fresh mint leaves |

Crust: Combine cookie crumbs and butter. Press onto bottom of 9 inch springform pan.

For filling: Combine 3 (8 ounce) packages cream cheese and sugar, mixing at medium speed on electric mixer until well blended. Add eggs, one at a time, mixing well after each addition. Blend in sour cream and vanilla. Pour over crust.

Combine remaining (8 ounce) package cream cheese and melted chocolate, mixing at medium speed until well blended. Add preserves. Mix well.

Drop rounded tablespoonfuls of chocolate raspberry cream cheese batter over plain cream cheese batter. Do not swirl. Bake at 325 degrees 1 hour and 20 minutes.

Loosen cake from rim of pan. Cool before removing rim of pan.

Melt remaining chocolate chips and whipping cream over low heat, stirring until smooth. Spread over cheesecake. Chill. Garnish with additional whipped cream, raspberries and fresh mint leaves.

## Uncle Bill's Cheesecake

### Crust

| | |
|---|---|
| 1 | package (1½ cups) graham crackers (crushed fine) |
| ⅓ | cup brown sugar |
| 7 | tablespoons melted butter or margarine |

### Filling

| | |
|---|---|
| 3 | (8 ounce) packages cream cheese |
| 1 | cup sugar |
| 1 | teaspoon vanilla |
| 4 | eggs |

Crust: Mix ingredients together and line 8½-inch foil cake pan with crust mixture.

Filling: Mix cream cheese, sugar, and vanilla together. Mix in one egg at a time until creamy. Pour into crust lined pan and bake 40-50 minutes. Should brown around the edges slightly. When the top starts to crack, remove from the oven. Center may still look uncooked when you remove from the oven. It will set when cooled. Let cool for 10-15 minutes and cover with plastic wrap. Refrigerate until cold.

Top with your fresh berries or cherry pie filling.

## Peach Amaretto Cobbler Crisp

| | |
|---|---|
| 2 | (8 ounce) packages frozen peaches |
| ½ | cup flour |
| 1 | cup sugar |
| ¼ | cup Amaretto |
| | nonstick cooking spray |
| ½ | cup uncooked oatmeal |
| ½ | cup butter |
| 1 | cup pecans |
| ½ | cup sugar |
| ½ | cup flour |
| | ice cream |

Preheat oven to 350 degrees. Defrost peaches. In large bowl, combine peaches, flour, sugar and Amaretto and mix well. Spray deep pie dish with nonstick cooking spray. Pour peach mixture into deep pie dish. In food processor, combine oatmeal, butter, pecans, sugar and flour. Mix until crumbly and sprinkle over entire peach mixture. Bake at 350 degrees for 45 to 60 minutes or until bubbly and slightly brown on top. Let cool slightly and serve with ice cream.

# Fall Harvest Pumpkin Roll

**Cake**

| | | |
|---|---|---|
| 1 | cup sugar |
| ⅔ | cup flour |
| 3 | eggs |
| ½ | teaspoon baking soda |
| ¾ | teaspoon cinnamon |
| ⅔ | cup pumpkin |

**Filling**

| | | |
|---|---|---|
| 1 | cup sifted powdered sugar |
| 1 | (8 ounce) package cream cheese |
| 6 | teaspoon butter |
| 1 | teaspoon vanilla |
| | powdered sugar for dusting |

Cake: Mix all ingredients together and pour into lightly greased and floured wax paper lined cookie sheet. Bake 15 minutes at 350 degrees.

Remove immediately and place on a tea towel that has been lightly dusted with powdered sugar. Peel off waxed paper. Roll up in tea towel until cool. When cake is cool, unroll and spread filling and roll up again.

Filling: Cream butter and cream cheese well. Slowly add powdered sugar, creaming well. Add vanilla and spread on cooled cake. Place in refrigerator several hours to set. When ready to serve, dust top lightly with sifted powdered sugar.

*May be frozen.*

# White Chocolate Tamales

| | | |
|---|---|---|
| 1 | pound white chocolate |
| ½ | cup pecan pieces |
| | corn husks for tamales |

Chop chocolate into small pieces and place in a mixing bowl over hot water. Let melt, stirring often. Do not get any water in chocolate. Add pecans and cool slightly. Run husks under hot water and wring to dry. Tear husks into three inch wide strips. Using a small spoon, place about 1 tablespoon mix in the center of tamale and roll up lengthwise. Let harden. Store in freezer until ready to serve.

231

# Peach Raspberry Batter Cake

Fruit Layer

| | | |
|---|---|---|
| ½ | cup sugar |
| 1½ | teaspoon cornstarch |
| 1 | (10 ounce) package frozen sliced peaches, thawed and drained well, reserving ⅓ cup of the syrup |
| 1 | tablespoon fresh lemon juice |
| 2 | cups red raspberries |

Batter

| | | |
|---|---|---|
| ½ | cup (1 stick) unsalted butter |
| ½ | cup sugar |
| 1 | large egg |
| 1 | teaspoon vanilla |
| 1 | cup all purpose flour |
| 1½ | teaspoon baking powder |
| ½ | cup milk |
| 1 | teaspoon grated lemon rind |
| | pinch salt |

Fruit Layer: In a heavy saucepan, combine the sugar and the cornstarch. Add reserved peach syrup and the lemon juice and combine the mixture well. Add peaches and red raspberries. Bring the liquid to a boil over moderate heat, stirring constantly. Simmer the mixture for 5 minutes. Remove pan from heat.

Batter: Lightly butter the baking dish and preheat oven to 350 degrees.

In a large bowl, with a mixer, cream the butter. Beat in the sugar, a little at a time, until light and fluffy. Add the egg and the vanilla and beat the mixture until smooth.

Sift together flour, baking powder and salt. Add flour mixture to the egg mixture in batches alternately with the milk, beating well after each addition. Stir in the lemon rind and blend the batter until smooth.

Spread the batter evenly in the baking dish. Spoon the peach-berry mixture over it and bake the dessert in the middle of the oven for 20 minutes. Reduce the heat to 325 degrees and bake the cake for 20 to 25 minutes more or until puffed and golden. Let the cake cool in the pan on a rack for 10 minutes and cut into squares.

# Ebony and Ivory Chocolate Truffles

Ivory Portion (white)

| | |
|---|---|
| 7½ | ounces white chocolate, chopped into ¼ inch pieces |
| ¼ | cup heavy cream |
| ½ | tablespoon sugar |
| ½ | tablespoon butter |

Ebony Portion (dark)

| | |
|---|---|
| 8 | ounces semisweet chocolate, chopped into ¼ inch pieces |
| ½ | cup heavy cream |
| ½ | tablespoon sugar |
| ½ | tablespoon butter |
| 6 | tablespoons good quality imported unsweetened cocoa |

Ivory Portion: Place the white chocolate into a stainless steel bowl. Heat the cream and sugar and butter in a heavy saucepan over medium high heat. Bring to a boil. Pour the boiling cream mixture over the chopped white chocolate. Allow to stand for 4 to 5 minutes. Whisk until smooth and creamy. Allow to cool for 1 hour at room temperature. Refrigerate for 15 minutes, stirring every 5 minutes. Set aside.

Ebony Portion: Place the dark chocolate into a stainless steel bowl. Heat the cream, sugar and butter in a heavy saucepan as above. Repeat all the steps. After the mixture has been refrigerated for the appropriate amount of time, drop by teaspoonfuls onto a cookie sheet that has been lined with parchment paper or waxed paper. Drop teaspoonfuls of white chocolate on top of the dark.

To fashion the truffles, roll each portion of chocolate that has been mounded on parchment in your palms in a gentle circular motion using just enough pressure to form smooth rounds. This will keep white on one side and dark on the other.

*Remember the chocolate will melt on contact with your hands, so this will be a tedious procedure to form the balls, but well worth the effort.*

Dip the rounds of chocolate in imported cocoa and roll until completely coated.

233

# After Dinner Peppermints

2 pounds white chocolate
1 pound peppermint
     candies, crushed

Melt chocolate over low heat, stirring till smooth. Remove from heat and stir in crushed candy. Spread on waxed paper on cookie sheets and chill 8 to 10 minutes. Break into pieces and store in airtight containers.
*For festive Christmas, use ½ red and ½ green candy. May use any crushed candy.*


# German Truffle Torte

1½ ounces bittersweet
     chocolate
2 ounces unsweetened
     chocolate
⅓ cup water
4 eggs
2 cups granulated sugar
½ cup cake flour
⅛ teaspoon salt
2 cups whipping cream
8 ounces shaved sweet
     chocolate
Red candied cherries

Cook chocolates with water until creamy. Add more water if necessary. Cool.

Beat eggs with sugar for 10 minutes at medium speed. Sift flour and salt over egg mixture. Fold over 5 times. Dribble chocolate mixture over and continue folding until combined. Bake at 350 degrees for 30 minutes in 2 slightly greased and floured 9 inch springform pans. Run knife around edge of pan. Invert on plate for 5 minutes.

Bring cream to a boil. Add shaved chocolate and stir to dissolve. Chill. Whip. Cover bottom layer, top and sides of torte with mixture. Trim outer edge with cherries, spacing each 1 inch apart.

234

# Hummingbird Cake with Cream Cheese Frosting

### Cake

| | |
|---|---|
| 3 | cups all purpose flour |
| 1 | teaspoon salt |
| 1 | teaspoon ground cinna-mon |
| 1½ | cups salad oil |
| 1 | (8 ounce) can crushed pineapple, undrained |
| 2 | cups chopped bananas |
| 2 | cups sugar |
| 1 | teaspoon baking soda |
| 3 | eggs, beaten |
| 1½ | teaspoons vanilla |
| 2 | cups chopped pecans |

### Frosting

| | |
|---|---|
| 2 | (8 ounce) packages cream cheese, softened |
| 2 | (16 ounce) boxes powdered sugar |
| 1 | cup margarine, softened |
| 2 | teaspoons vanilla |

Cake: Combine dry ingredients in large mixing bowl. Add eggs and salad oil, stirring until dry ingredients are moistened. Do not beat. Stir in vanilla, pineapple, pecans and bananas. Spoon batter into 3 well greased and floured 9 inch cake pans. Bake at 350 degrees for 25-30 minutes or until cake tests done. Cool in pans for 10 minutes. Remove from pans and cool completely. Frost when completely cool.

Frosting: Combine cream cheese and margarine. Cream until smooth. Add powdered sugar, beating until light and fluffy. Stir in vanilla.

# Coconut-Macadamia Nut Pound Cake

1½  cups butter, softened
3    cups sugar
6    large eggs
2½  cups all purpose flour
2    teaspoons baking powder
½    teaspoon salt
1½  cups buttermilk
2    cups flaked coconut
1    can macadamia nuts, a
      few reserved to chop in
      half and sprinkle on top
2    teaspoons vanilla extract
¼    cup coconut

Beat butter at medium speed with electric mixer about 2 minutes or until soft and creamy. Gradually add 3 cups sugar, beating at medium speed 5 to 7 minutes. Add eggs, one at a time, beating just until yellow disappears.

Combine flour and next 3 ingredients. Add to butter mixture alternately with buttermilk, beginning and ending with flour mixture. Mix at low speed just until blended after each addition.

Stir in coconut and vanilla. Blend well. Add macadamia nuts (except reserved nuts).

Pour batter into a greased and floured 10 inch tube pan. Sprinkle ¼ cup coconut and reserved macadamia nuts on top and bake at 350 degrees for 50 minutes. Cover loosely with aluminum foil to prevent excessive browning. Bake an additional 45 to 50 minutes or until a wooden pick inserted in center of cake comes out clean. Cool in pan on a wire rack 10 to 15 minutes. Remove from pan and let cool completely.

# Bourbon Pecan Pound Cake

Cake

| | |
|---|---|
| 1 | cup shortening |
| 2½ | cups sugar |
| 6 | large eggs |
| 1 | (8 ounce) carton sour cream |
| ½ | cup bourbon |
| 3 | cups all-purpose flour |
| 2 | teaspoons baking powder |
| ½ | teaspoon salt |
| ½ | teaspoon ground nutmeg |
| 1 | cup finely chopped pecans |

Glaze

| | |
|---|---|
| 2¼ | cups sifted powdered sugar |
| 2 | tablespoons bourbon |
| 2 | tablespoons water |

Beat shortening at medium speed with electric mixer until fluffy. Gradually add sugar, beating at medium speed 5 to 7 minutes. Add eggs, one at a time, beating just until yellow disappears.

Combine sour cream and ½ cup bourbon.

Combine flour and next 3 ingredients. Add to shortening mixture alternately with sour cream mixture, beginning and ending with flour mixture. Mix at low speed just until blended after each addition. Stir in pecans.

Pour batter into a greased and floured 10 inch tube pan.

Bake at 325 degrees for 1 hour and 10 to 15 minutes or until a wooden pick inserted in center comes out clean.

Cool in pan on a wire rack 10 to 15 minutes. Remove from pan and cool completely on wire rack. Drizzle with Bourbon Glaze.

Bourbon Glaze: Combine all ingredients, stirring until smooth.

# Five-Flavor Pound Cake

Cake

|   |   |
|---|---|
| 1 | cup butter or margarine, softened |
| ½ | cup shortening |
| 3 | cups sugar |
| 5 | large eggs |
| 3¼ | cups cake flour, sifted |
| ½ | teaspoon baking powder |
| ½ | teaspoon salt |
| 1 | cup milk |
| 1 | teaspoon vanilla extract |
| ½ | teaspoon lemon extract |
| ½ | teaspoon rum flavoring |
| ½ | teaspoon coconut flavoring |

Glaze

|   |   |
|---|---|
| ½ | cup sugar |
| ⅓ | cup water |
| ½ | teaspoon almond extract |

Cake: Beat butter and shortening at medium speed with an electric mixer about 2 minutes or until creamy. Gradually add sugar, beating at medium speed 5 to 7 minutes. Add eggs, one at a time, beating just until yellow disappears.

Combine flour, baking powder and salt. Add to butter mixture alternately with milk, beginning and ending with flour mixture. Mix at low speed just until blended after each addition. Stir in flavorings. Pour batter into a greased and floured 10 inch tube pan.

Bake at 325 degrees for 1 hour and 30 minutes or until a wooden pick inserted in center comes out clean. Cool in pan 10 minutes. Remove from pan and place on wire rack. Spoon Glaze over cake while warm. Cool completely on wire rack.

Glaze: Combine sugar and water in a small saucepan. Bring to a boil over medium heat. Remove from heat. Stir in almond extract.

# Peanut Butter Fudge Cake

**Cake**

| | |
|---|---|
| 2 | cups sugar |
| 2 | cups plain flour, sifted |
| 1 | teaspoon baking soda |
| 2 | sticks margarine |
| 2 | eggs |
| 4 | tablespoons cocoa |
| 1 | cup water |
| 1 | cup buttermilk |
| 1 | teaspoon vanilla |
| 1½ | cup whipped peanut butter |

**Fudge Frosting**

| | |
|---|---|
| 1 | stick margarine |
| 4 | tablespoons cocoa |
| 6 | tablespoons buttermilk |
| 1 | box sifted powdered sugar |
| 1 | teaspoon vanilla |

Cake: Bring to a boil the margarine, cocoa, water and buttermilk. Pour over sifted flour and soda. Mix well with spoon. Add two beaten eggs and 1 teaspoon vanilla. Pour into well greased shallow baking pan, 13x9-inch or larger. Bake at 350 degrees for 25 minutes. Cool in pan.

Warm 1½ cups peanut butter to spreading consistency and spread on cold cake. Cool again and cover with icing.

Fudge Frosting: Bring margarine, cocoa and buttermilk to a boil. Pour over powdered sugar and vanilla. Mix and spread on cake.

# Cranberry Cake with Butter Sauce

**Cake**

| | |
|---|---|
| 2 | cups flour, sifted |
| 1 | cup sugar |
| 2 | teaspoons baking powder |
| ½ | teaspoon salt |
| 1 | cup milk |
| 2 | teaspoons melted butter |
| 2 | cups whole cranberries |

**Butter Sauce**

| | |
|---|---|
| ½ | cup butter |
| 1 | cup white or brown sugar |
| ¾ | cup cream |

Cake: Mix all ingredients. Pour into two greased and floured 9 inch round cake pans. Bake at 350 degrees for 30 minutes. Cut in wedges and spoon hot butter sauce over individual pieces.

Butter Sauce: Melt butter in saucepan. Add sugar and cream. Bring to boiling point and cook for 10 minutes. Serve hot.

# Quick, Easy and Sinfully Rich Chocolate Cake

10 ounces bittersweet or semisweet chocolate, chopped (not unsweetened)
1 cup unsalted butter, cut into small pieces
5 large eggs
1¼ cups sugar
⅓ cup cake flour
1½ teaspoons baking powder
powdered sugar for dusting
½ pint whipping cream, whipped
1 tablespoon sugar
1 pint fresh strawberries, halved or 1 pint raspberries

Preheat oven to 325 degrees. Butter and flour a 10 inch springform pan with 2¼ inch sides. Stir chocolate and butter in heavy saucepan over low heat until chocolate melts and mixture is smooth.

Beat eggs and 1¼ cups sugar in large bowl until well blended and beginning to thicken. Sift flour and baking powder over eggs and fold in. Gradually fold in the chocolate mixture. Pour batter into prepared pan.

Bake cake for 20 minutes. Cover pan with foil and continue baking until tester inserted into center comes out with moist crumbs still attached or about 30 minutes longer. Uncover cake. Cool in pan on wire rack. Cake will fall as it cools.

Cut around pan sides to loosen cake. Release pan sides. Sift powdered sugar over cake and decorate with strawberries or raspberries. Serve with whipped cream sprinkled with cinnamon, if desired. Cut into wedges.

240

*Photo on right ~*
Petit Pots de Crème au
Chocolat, page 217

# Irish Cream Chocolate Cake

1  package Devil's food cake mix
1  small package instant chocolate pudding
2  cups sour cream
4  eggs
¾  cup oil
½  cup Irish crème liqueur
1  cup chocolate chips

Combine all ingredients except chocolate chips. Fold in chocolate chips. Bake in well greased bundt pan at 350 degrees for one hour. Dust with powdered sugar when cool. Serve with whipped cream.

*Substitute coffee liqueur for Irish crème liqueur.*

# Williamsburg Pecan Pie

1  unbaked pie shell
1  cup pecans, chopped or in halves
1  teaspoon vanilla
1½  cup white corn syrup
¾  cup sugar
4  eggs
1  tablespoon melted butter
   pinch salt

Preheat oven to 400 degrees. Spread pecans on bottom of unbaked pie shell. Combine remaining ingredients in bowl with spoon. Pour over pecans. Place in oven and immediately reduce heat to 350 degrees. Bake for 40 to 50 minutes until center is firm.

# Lemon Chess Pie

1½  cups sugar
4  teaspoons cornstarch
2  teaspoons fresh lemon peel, finely grated
4  eggs
⅓  cup lemon juice
5  tablespoons unsalted butter, melted and cooled
1  9 inch pie crust, partially baked

Preheat oven to 325 degrees. Combine sugar and cornstarch in large bowl and mix, pressing out any lumps. Stir in lemon juice. Blend in butter. Pour filling into pie shell. Bake until puffed and golden brown, 50 to 60 minutes. Cool to room temperature before serving.

*Photo on left ~*
Icebound by Gas Logs, page 18

*Accessories Courtesy*
*Haltom's Jewelers*

241

## Chocolate Pecan Pie

| | |
|---|---|
| 2 | cups sugar |
| 2 | sticks margarine |
| 6 | eggs, slightly beaten |
| 2 | cups chopped pecans |
| ½ | cup self-rising flour |
| 8 | cubes chocolate bark (or 2 squares unsweetened chocolate) |
| 2 | teaspoons vanilla |

Melt butter and chocolate over double boiler. Beat in eggs and vanilla. Add pecans. Pre-bake pie crust for 5 to 10 minutes. Then pour mixture into pie crust. Bake at 350 degrees for 35 to 40 minutes.


## French Coconut Pie

| | |
|---|---|
| 1½ | cups sugar |
| ½ | cup butter |
| 3 | eggs, separated |
| 1 | tablespoon flour |
| 1 | tablespoon corn meal |
| 1½ | teaspoons white vinegar |
| 1½ | cups coconut |
| 1 | uncooked pie shell |

Cream sugar and butter. Add flour, corn meal, egg yolks and vinegar. Mix well. Beat egg whites until they begin to turn white. Fold egg whites and coconut into cream mixture. Pour into pie shell. Bake at 325 degrees for 30 minutes.


## Margarita Pie

| | |
|---|---|
| 1 | (14 ounce) can sweetened condensed milk |
| 5 | tablespoons tequila |
| 5 | tablespoons triple sec |
| ½ | cup freshly squeezed lime juice |
| 1½ | cups whipping cream, beaten until stiff |
| | graham cracker crust for 9- or 10-inch pie |

Blend together condensed milk, tequila, triple sec, and lime juice. Fold in whipped cream. Pour into graham cracker crust and freeze for four hours until firm. Serve garnished with whipped cream and slice of lime.

242

# Pineapple Icebox Dessert

Dessert

| | |
|---|---|
| ¾ | cup crushed vanilla wafers |
| ½ | cup soft butter or margarine |
| 1½ | cups sifted confectioners' sugar |
| 1 | egg, beaten |
| 1 | (1 pound, 4 ounce) can crushed pineapple |
| ⅔ | cups pecans, coarsely chopped |
| 1 | cup heavy cream, whipped |
| | Pineapple sauce (below), optional |

Pineapple Sauce

| | |
|---|---|
| ½ | cup sugar |
| 1 | tablespoon cornstarch |
| ¼ | teaspoon grated lemon peel |
| 1 | (8 ounce) can crushed pineapple |

Day before serving: Lightly grease 8-inch square cake pan. Pack half the crumbs in bottom of pan.

In medium bowl, with wooden spoon, cream butter and sugar until fluffy. Add egg, beating well. Drain pineapple well, reserving syrup for Pineapple Sauce. Fold in pineapple and pecans. Fold in whipped cream just until well combined.

Turn into prepared pan, spreading evenly. Sprinkle with rest of crumbs. Cover top of pan with foil or plastic film. Refrigerate 24 hours. Cut in squares. Serve with sauce, if desired.

Pineapple Sauce: In small saucepan, combine sugar and cornstarch. Mix well. Measure reserved pineapple syrup (above) and, if necessary, add water to make ¾ cup. Gradually ad pineapple juice, stirring until smooth. Add lemon peel and crushed pineapple. Bring to boiling over medium heat, stirring. Boil until mixture is thickened and translucent. Cover and refrigerate. Serves 8-10

# Kahlúa and Praline Brownies

Praline Crust
- ⅓ cup firmly packed light brown sugar
- 5⅓ tablespoons butter
- ⅔ cup all purpose flour
- ½ cup finely chopped pecans

Brownie Filling
- 2 ounces (2 squares) unsweetened chocolate
- ¼ cup solid vegetable shortening
- 4 tablespoons butter
- ¼ cup granulated sugar
- ½ cup firmly packed light brown sugar
- 1 teaspoon vanilla extract
- 2 large eggs
- ¼ cup Kahlúa liqueur
- ½ cup all purpose flour
- ¼ teaspoon salt
- ½ cup chopped pecans

Kahlúa Butter Cream Frosting
- 2 tablespoons soft butter
- 2 cups sifted confectioners sugar
- 1 tablespoon Kahlúa liqueur
- 1 tablespoon cream

Praline crust: Mix together brown sugar, butter, flour and pecans. Pat evenly in bottom of 9-inch square baking pan. Set aside.

Preheat oven to 350 degrees. In large saucepan, melt chocolate with shortening and butter over low heat. Remove from heat, cool 5 minutes. Beat in sugars and vanilla. Add the eggs one at a time while beating. Stir in Kahlúa. Add the flour and salt, mixing into a smooth batter. Fold in pecans. Pour into the pan lined with praline crust and bake 25 minutes, being careful not to overbake. Let cool in pan.

Frosting: Beat all ingredients until smooth and creamy. If necessary, beat in additional Kahlúa for a good spreading consistency. Spread frosting over top of brownies. Place in refrigerator ½ hour to set before cutting squares. Makes 3 dozen

# Macadamia Bars

Crust

| | | |
|---|---|---|
| ½ | cup butter, softened |
| ¼ | cup sugar |
| 1 | cup all-purpose flour |

Filling

| | |
|---|---|
| 2 | large eggs, lightly beaten |
| ½ | cup sweetened flaked coconut |
| 1½ | cups packed light brown sugar |
| 1-1½ | cups halved macadamia nuts |
| 2 | tablespoons all-purpose flour |
| 1½ | teaspoons pure vanilla extract |
| ½ | teaspoon baking powder |

In medium bowl, cream together all crust ingredients. Press onto bottom of 9-inch square pan and bake at 350 degrees for 20 minutes.

In medium bowl, stir together all filling ingredients. Pour over hot baked crust and bake at 350 degrees for an additional 20 minutes. Cool completely and cut into squares. Makes 16-20 bars

*Moist, chewy and absolutely sinful. Great served with vanilla ice cream.*

# Simple Sesames

| | |
|---|---|
| 2 | cups (1 pound) butter, softened |
| 1½ | cups sugar |
| 3 | cups all purpose flour |
| 1 | cup sesame seed |
| 2 | cups shredded coconut |
| ½ | cup finely chopped almonds |

In large mixing bowl, cream butter. Gradually add sugar and continue beating until light and fluffy. Add flour and mix just until combined. Stir in sesame seed, coconut and almonds just until well mixed. Divide dough into thirds. Place one third on long sheet of wax paper. Shape into a long roll 2 inches in diameter. Repeat with remaining dough. Wrap and refrigerate until firm.

Preheat oven to 300 degrees. Cut rolls into ¼ inch slices. Bake on ungreased cookie sheets 30 minutes. Remove to wire racks to cool. Makes 4 dozen

245

# Microwave Bananas Foster

¼  cup butter
¼  cup brown sugar firmly
     packed
2  tablespoons white corn
     syrup
½  teaspoon rum extract
¼  teaspoon cinnamon
2  bananas
   ice cream or frozen yogurt

In an uncovered 1½ to 2 quart microwave safe bowl, heat all ingredients (except bananas) for 1 minute on high. Slice the bananas while the other ingredients are cooking. Stir the mixture and cook for 1 minute more. Add the bananas to the sauce and microwave 40 seconds. Spoon over vanilla ice cream or frozen yogurt. Serves 4

*This can be prepared while the coffee is being made. It has been made for 8 people with very little waiting.*

246

Acknowledgments

# Acknowledgments

We would like to express our sincere appreciation to the members of the Colleyville Woman's Club and their families and friends for all the hours of sharing recipes, testing recipes, and tasting the fruits of their efforts over and over. Our two presidents who were involved in the effort: Karen Cantrell who encouraged us in our early stages and Shirley Schollmeyer, who has cheered us on through the tough times and has shared our victories. Our faithful fund raiser vice president Sue Howery has not only lent her support and time, but even lent her home for several of our events.

We give our heartfelt thanks to the following people without whose contributions this cookbook would not be all it has become:

• To Dian Thompson Chandler for being a catalyst to the community and encouraging them to embrace this project.

• To Bruce Graham and Ladye Ann Rowe of Haltom's Jewelers for contributing financially as well as lending their beautiful merchandise for our photographs. They trusted us with a set of Herend china, including the gorgeous soup tureen featured in our soup photo.

• To Nancy Barry and Diane Scurlock of the Dallas Morning News for their expertise and guidance. While we appreciate their financial contributions, we value their personal attention to us even more.

• To the wonderful artists and staff at Greg Booth and Associates: Allie Frankfort who listened to our dream and helped make it a reality; Carol Booth who created such a positive experience for us; Dave Carlin, our photographer whose creativity, professionalism, and sense of humor made our days with him sheer pleasure; his assistant Nathan Shroder who did a lot of the unseen tasks; Jackie Forster and her husband Bill, our food stylist who not only created beautiful food but also recreated some of our recipes; Mandy Mitchell who helped us find our way around her kitchen; and Amber Sweatt who even contributed real bluebonnets from her garden.

• To Albertson's Food and Drug Stores for food for our photo shoot, to Flowers in Bloom for the floral arrangements, to Redenta's Garden Center for loaning items for our "Bloom Where You're Planted" photograph, to Cavendar Boots for the boots on the back cover, and to Pier One Imports for loaning the merchandise we used in several shots.

Sincerely,

Judith Eulberg
Debra Schneider
Lynda Sanders
Jean Neisius

# Financial Supporters

We would like to say a special "thank you" to the following for their support of our project through a financial donation or goods or services to help make this project a success.

## Underwriting Benefactors

The Dallas Morning News
Haltom's Jewelers
Greg Booth and Associates

## Patrons of Colleyville Woman's Club

Arp-Lotter Investments and Tampico Citrus Punch
Davis Foundation
Landmark Bank
Baylor Medical Center

## Circle of Giving

Bedford Imaging, Inc.
Q-Imaging Plus, Inc.
Colleyville News and Times

## Circle of Hope

Red Star Yeast and Products
Judy and Gilbert Duncan
Grand Prairie State Bank

## Friends of Colleyville Woman's Club

Adolescent and Pediatric Orthopedics, P.A.
Quantum Computer Concepts
Paul Straten, Inc.
Specialty Orthopedics, P.A.
Albertson's Food and Drug Stores
Cyrano Antiques
Flowers in Bloom
Redenta's Garden
Pier 1 Imports
Rsvp
Cavendar Boots
Christine Pasienski
Chase Bank of Texas

249

# Contributors

Anne Adams
Marguerite Alexander
Lawan Andersen
Barbara Antczak
Jim Antczak
Donna Arp
Kerry Avery
Carole Battist
Mary Beadles
Karen Birkes
Rachel Bowling
Sally Bracey
Janet Cady
Karen Cantrell
Cheryl Cardon
Sheila Carter
Karen Chapman
Claudia Ann Cimma
Barbara Clark
Terry Cosmano
Kay Craft
Debbie Craig
Martha Cucci
Beverley Dalton
Nancy Dennis
Donna Bills DeOrozco
Jane Deupree
Roseann DiCostanzo
Audrey Dusendschon
Amy Ellison
Rosalyn Ellison
Judith Eulberg
Marti Eulberg
Pat Eulberg
Bonnie Everhart
Nancy Farrar
Jan Fisher
Gloria Flores
Diane Foia
Nancy Foley
Sandie Fouke
Florence Gambino
Terri Gill
Cathy Gordon
Sue Gordon
Lorah Gough

Connie Grady
Suzanne Harrington
Janie Helling
De Ette Hoch
Karen Hodges
Mary Hollech
Barbara Holliday
Lea Ann Holsteen
Belinda Hovland
Sue Howery
Cheri Irwin
Patti Irwin
Dann Isley
Kelly Karl
John King,
    Executive Chef
Jill Kralicke
Meredith Krebel
Bonnie Kurtz
Catherine LaCroix
Vicki Leech
Mary Leeper
Dave Lieber
Faye Loftis
Susan Loftis
William Maddox
Mrs. Bill Magnan
Rebecca Manning
Mary Martin
Phyllis Masalkoski
Elizabeth Mattson
Charleen McClain
Mary McClain
Lucille McCormick
Karen McWhorter
Bianca Mierkiewicz
Susan Miller
Judy Moist
Mary Mullen
Dot Munger
Pamela Nee
Jean Neisius
Jane Nelson
Nichola Niemi
Becci Nooney
Sharon O'Neil

Kay O'Shaughnessy
Beryl Palmer
Bonnie Pasienski
Michelle Paul
Mary Pierce
Norma Pletzke
Lillian Porter
Judy Pratt
Dan Prebish
Kay Priest
Mae Priest
Carol Provost
Debbie Reeder
Sandy Robinson
Billie Jo Runyon
Lynda Sanders
Debra Schneider
Shirley Schollmeyer
Susan Seal
Helen See
Susan Segee
Diane Segel
Leah Shaver
Andrea Sherwin
Syble Shoults
Brenda Shriver
Jill Slesinski
Debbie Smith
Emogene Smith
Janet Smith
Shirley Orr Smith
Tom Smith
Lonna Souther
Gene-Marie Sperduti
Marilyn Starkey
Charla Stringer
Sharon Taylor
Jaime Thibodeaux
Ginny Tigue
Laura Travis
Karen Vazquez
Linda Welch
Royce Welch
Judith Wills
Cindy Woelke
Maurine Wood

250

# Index

258

## Black Tie and Boots Optional
### Colleyville Woman's Club
P.O. Box 181
Colleyville, Texas 76034

Please send _____copies of

| | | |
|---|---|---|
| Black Tie and Boots Optional | @ $19.95 each | _____ |
| Postage and handling | @ 3.50 each | _____ |
| Texas residents add 7.75% sales tax | @ 1.55 each | _____ |
| | TOTAL | _____ |

Name _____

Address _____

City _____ State _____ Zip _____

*Make check payable to Colleyville Woman's Club*

- - - - - - - - - - - - - - - - - - - - - - - - - - - - - - - - - - -

## Black Tie and Boots Optional
### Colleyville Woman's Club
P.O. Box 181
Colleyville, Texas 76034

Please send _____copies of

| | | |
|---|---|---|
| Black Tie and Boots Optional | @ $19.95 each | _____ |
| Postage and handling | @ 3.50 each | _____ |
| Texas residents add 7.75% sales tax | @ 1.55 each | _____ |
| | TOTAL | _____ |

Name _____

Address _____

City _____ State _____ Zip _____

*Make check payable to Colleyville Woman's Club*

- - - - - - - - - - - - - - - - - - - - - - - - - - - - - - - - - - -

## Black Tie and Boots Optional
### Colleyville Woman's Club
P.O. Box 181
Colleyville, Texas 76034

Please send _____copies of

| | | |
|---|---|---|
| Black Tie and Boots Optional | @ $19.95 each | _____ |
| Postage and handling | @ 3.50 each | _____ |
| Texas residents add 7.75% sales tax | @ 1.55 each | _____ |
| | TOTAL | _____ |

Name _____

Address _____

City _____ State _____ Zip _____

*Make check payable to Colleyville Woman's Club*